3,500/-

asian
architects

GÜLSÜM B. NALBANTOGLU

PAUL CARTER

GEOFFREY BAWA

TAO HO

ERNESTO BEDMAR

CHARLES CORREA

SEUNG H. SANG

RAHUL MEHROTRA

WILLIAM S. W. LIM

NEVZAT SAYIN

CHANG YUNG HO

LIM TENG NGIOM

SEAN GODSELL

With a Foreword by Kenneth Frampton

ASIAN architects

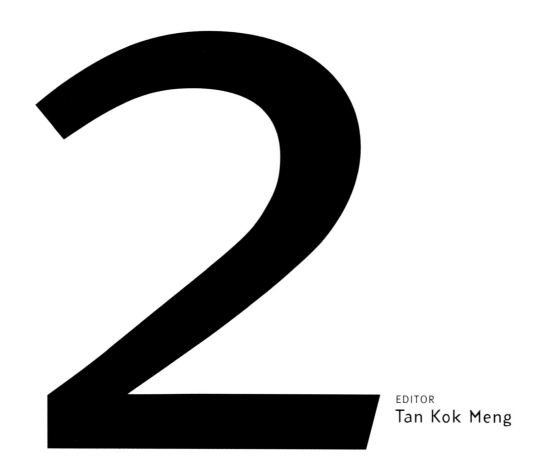

2

EDITOR
Tan Kok Meng

SELECT PUBLISHING

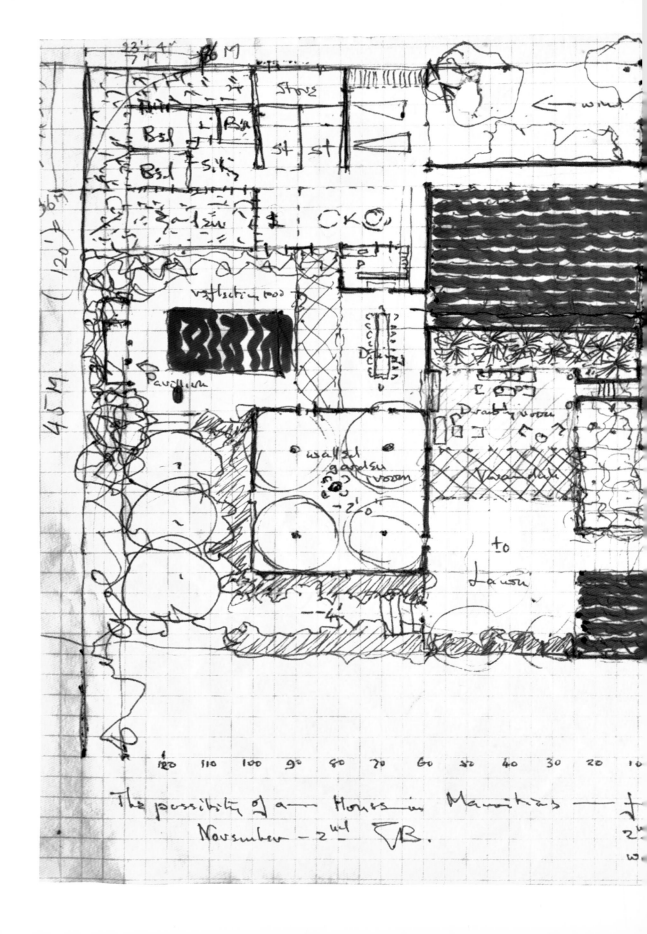

13'-4"
7 M
6 M

Store

Bed   L   R"
       st   st
Bed   Sik

Garden $ CKO
                    P

reflection pool

Pavilion

walled
garden room
      2' 0"

Dining

Drawing room

Veranda

to
Lawn

120 110 100 9⁰ 8⁰ 7⁰ 6⁰ 5⁰ 4⁰ 3⁰ 2⁰ 1⁰

36 M
(120')

45 M

The possibility of a House in Mauritius —
November - 2ⁿᵈ JB.

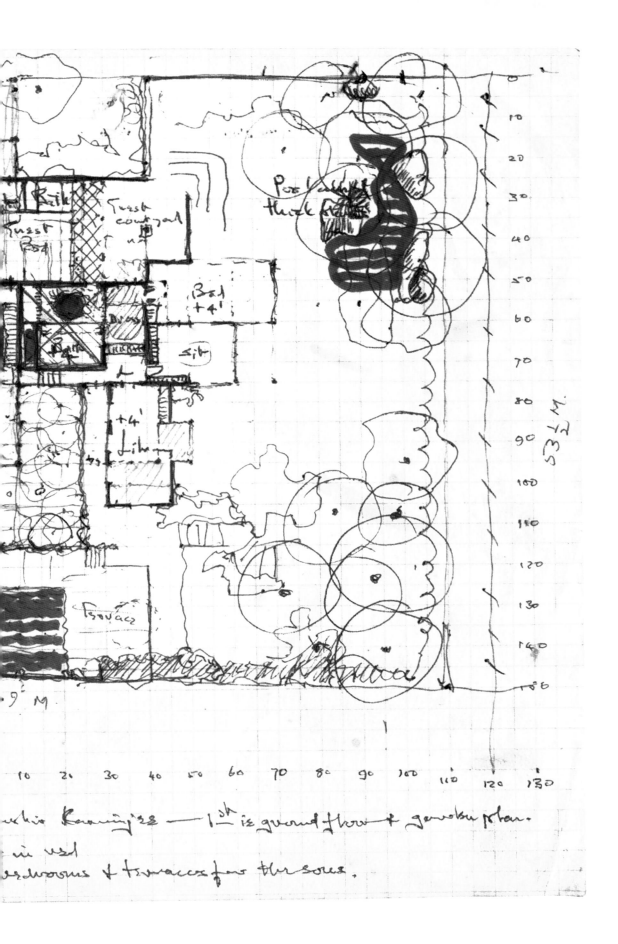

Brk

Guest
courtyard

Guest
Pod

Pot planter
thick planter

Bed
+4'

Dress

Bath

Sit

+4'
Lib

Terrace

0

10

20

30

40

50

60

70

80

90

100

110

120

130

140

150

53 M.

9 M.

10   20   30   40   50   60   70   80   90   100   110   120   130

this drawing '88 — 1st is ground floor + garden plan.
in red
bedrooms + terraces for the sons.

Cover picture: Marine Parade Community Club by William Lim Associates.
Frontispieces:
Pages 4 & 5: Initial sketch by Geoffrey Bawa for the Currimjee House in Curepipe Mauritius.
Pages 8 & 9: Vidhan Bhavan, State Assembly by Charles Correa.

Asia witnessed a remarkable political, economic and social transformation in the post-war years. Many countries have progressed from agrarian-based colonial territories to independent nations with fast-growth industrial economies. This development is paralleled most evidently in the built environment, dramatically transforming the cityscapes of many Asian cities.

Notwithstanding the present economic turbulence in Asia, its rapid economic growth has also ushered in a shift in the balance of power along cultural lines. There is widely in place a confident affirmation of the cultural content of its indigenous societies and a coming to terms with its colonial pasts. Architecture, when understood as the production of cultural ideas in spatial terms, resolutely locates itself in such positions.

The Asian Architects series attempts to record this physical and thus cultural/aesthetic transformation and tries to reveal the creative processes that produced it. The series documents the creative works of Asian architects or architects working in the Asian context, whose works deserve a wider international exposure. As the material that is currently available is inadequate, dispersed, or not readily available, this series aims to be a primary source of information about architecture in Asia upon which further research can be conducted. Finally, it hopes to set the tone for sharpening architectural discourse and critical appreciation of architecture in Asia.

The series has an Advisory Committee comprising leading Asian architects. They are: Charles Correa, Tao Ho, Sumet Jumsai, William S. W. Lim, Fumihiko Maki, Leon van Schaik and Wu Liangyong.

The publishers are also guided by a Working Committee in Singapore, comprising

Publisher's Preface

William S. W. Lim, Mok Wei Wei, Robert Powell, Tan Hock Beng, Tang Guan Bee and Tan Kok Meng. Guest editors are invited to work on different volumes.

One of the major problems encountered was to define the parameters of such a series. What are the imaginary boundaries that the term Asia encompasses? What criteria should be used for the inclusion or exclusion of certain architects or works of architecture? Albeit potentially inviting controversy, for the purpose of manageability this series covers geographical bounds from Turkey in the west, to the Philippines in the east, from South Korea in the north to Australia in the south.

The inclusion of Australia in this series is somewhat timely. Sharing a common "post-colonial" experience with places like Malaysia, Singapore, India and Indonesia, Australia, in recent years, has continually looked askance at traditional sources of cultural influence from Europe and North America, to examine from within, authentic sources of its own physical and cultural experiences. Leon van Schaik, a South African born, British trained, Australian academic, writing about his own particular experience in this series has made claims for a vital dialectical relationship between what he calls the "Metropolis" and the "Province". These terms correspond respectively to the predominant spheres of architectural discourse and those from the subordinate hinterlands. The flow of ideas from the "Metropolis" to the "Province" is not the conventionally regarded unilateral one, but encompasses a complex interconnectivity that distresses simple reduction. Framed in this way, Australia clearly sites itself in the "Province" together with the rest of Asia. It is this shared concern for exerting a concerted effort together with their Asian counterparts to offer alternative discourses that Australian architects are firmly aligned with the Asians in this series.

Japan, however, is excluded from the first six volumes of this series. It is felt that it has emerged over the years as a major source of architectural discourse through its high standard of professional achievement and its reputable international publications which include extensive documentation of Japanese works of architecture.

Each of the six volumes will feature the works and thoughts of leading Asian architects whose bodies of work are well respected by the architectural community at large. Also included are younger architects whose works show much promise. Twelve architects will be featured in each volume. Their selection for publication is purely contrived to bring together a good mix of unique approaches from different geographical regions.

The series also discusses what are perceived as important issues/topics confronting architecture and urbanism in Asia with the aim to provoke discussion. They are:

• The metropolis and province
• Writing post-coloniality
• Sustainable architecture
• Contemporary vernacular
• The new Asian architecture and urbanism
• Modernity and tradition

The publishers had the wholehearted support of the Advisory Committee, and benefited from their wise counsel on the content and direction of the series. Meetings with the Working Committee were always long, demanding, challenging and rewarding. The publishers record their thanks and appreciation to every member of both committees for their invaluable contributions in making this a meaningful publishing experience, and this series a reality. And to the contributing architects, thank you for your willingness to be a part of this series and your patience in meeting our constant calls for additional materials.

Select Publishing is indeed pleased and privileged to be able to add to the growing literature on architecture in Asia.

Select Publishing

Behind the selection of architects for all the intended volumes of *Asian Architect*, is the desire to present a diverse range of approaches and works of architects and architectural educators from the Asian region, including Australia. The grouping of these architects into various volumes is rather arbitrary, motivated more by the need for an even geographical representation. Other than that, there is no attempt to group them based on conceptual or thematic similarities. Therefore the reader is urged to be aware that the comments made here about the architects featured in this volume are considerably reductive, simplistic and in no way depict the complexities and intricacies layered in their work. They are framed quickly in the manner below simply to allow a way to get into the works.

The search for a more qualitative urban environment in Asia has always been simultaneously championed by marginal local voices during the sustained period of greed and quantitative projects in Asian countries undergoing rapid economic development in recent years. Now making inroads into mainstream consciousness, there is a boosted ambition tinged with much anxiety in Asia to recover a local Asian specificity to counter the perceived fear of homogenisation brought on by the forces of globalisation.

Across Asia, this is enacted with different degrees of sophistication and persuasion. Often, the universalising tendencies of a connected global situation are cast reductively as decadent thus 'bad' 'Western' influences, because they predominantly originate from the US and Europe, that through their associative forces – modernisation of society and urbanisation of the built environment – bring about erosion and replacement of the physical and ideological structures of traditional Asian societies. And it does not matter even if some of these forces are obviously not from the 'West'. For instance, Japan's significant role in the process of globalisation of economies is selectively forgotten; whilst other newly established secondary players to this process, such as South Korea, Singapore, Taiwan and Hong Kong (SAR) which have all begun to pour investments into other Asian countries, are also ignored since they do not fit into the reductive East-West binary.

Introduction

In the architectural world in Asia, perhaps as a reaction to the hegemonic processes of the 'West', models that are non-'Western' are consciously held up, especially if these are also to be sanctioned by Western architectural media. In her essay published in this volume, Gülsüm Baydar Nalbatoglu warns that privileging one term over the other in this binary pairing (West and non-West) serves only to keep this bipolarisation intact. They are opposite sides of the same coin.

Indeed, as she asks rhetorically, "has there been architectural theory outside the West?" we see retrospectively that there was a great amount of instrumentality in the way that only architectures that could either act as exemplars that relied on eurocentric architectural values or diametrically opposed to those same values were included in the official accounts of architectural histories from the West. Non-Western architectures were continuously idealised in these histories. There was an attempt too in the mid 60's to incoporate the Japanese Metabolist movement in a similar manner, which saw Europeans for the first time giving serious attention to modern architectural developments in Asia. Of course it was always going to be more convoluted than that: the megastructural tendencies of the Metabolists coincided, influenced and were in turn influenced by the megastructuralism in vogue in Europe at that time. Reyner Banham's 1976 version of that story is only belatedly complimented by the recent account given from the 'other' side by Hajime Yatsuka and Hideki Yoshimatsu in their new book, written in Japanese, about the movement (*Metabolism: Japanese Avant garde Architecture in the Sixties*, INAX Shyuppan, 1997).

Another instance of incorporation of Asian (strictly in geographical terms) architecture into Western discourse after the 1960s: the reconsolidation of humanistic 'identity' discourses in architecture after the loss of faith in abstract universal Modernism; from segmenting the Western architectural world into different 'regions' to Frampton's Critical Regionalism, circa 1980s, in which he systematises a critical and therefore authentic modern architecture inflected by appropriate responses to climatic, topographic, and cultural-tectonic contexts. From Asia, he cites the work of Tadao Ando (amongst other European and even American examples), for his insistence on a "closed modern architecture... [which] is likely to alter with the region in which it sends out roots and grows in various distinctive individual ways, still, though closed." The dialectics implied in Critical Regionalism was much missed by many, who invoked the label in vain, reviving certain cultural traditions in a much too direct and pastiched fashion. Many Asian architects could not see the problem of relying on already non-vital past cultures – fossilised and essentialised for ideological purposes – as reinforcement of authentic identity.

There are however, other forms of qualitative projects of Asian architecture. And some are showcased in this volume.

The work of Geoffrey Bawa has often been held up as an exemplar of how an authentic, identifiably 'Asian' architecture might be defined through the adaptation of traditional culture. The flip side of course is that often Bawa is reduced to a 'style': how Asian architecture should look. Often missed is the dialectical relationship between the old and the new, the found and the made; and the economic, cultural besides the physical contexts in which Bawa and his work are so embedded.

Bawa's 'mastery' lies in his acutely sensitive way in which an architecture of emotive spaces is moulded simultaneously to be part of and to stand apart from its physical context; an intervention that marks a strong presence yet at the same time is harmoniously included within the site in which it sits. A manifesto-like work of his particular approach would be the Cinnamon Hill guest house at the southern end of Bawa's Lunuganga compound. There, he developed the plan by physically stretching strings on pegs around existing trees in situ. Eventually, only one tree was cut, and this became the base for a table in the new pavilion structure. Bawa's impulse to preserve is mediated by expedient pragmatism; the cut tree stump takes on another useful role.

This dialectical conservationist attitude towards the site is also extended to the architecture: two 18th century windows that he was given were incorporated into the new structure. The old windows are used again on top of their obviously aesthetic-symbolic function. Old architectural elements from a past architectural tradition in this case are conserved and re-used, presenting a richly textured and complex relationship between new and old. And his statements published in this volume succinctly paint the nuances of his thinking process towards the completely subjective yet highly practical, concrete attitude of the building process. This is how, as Baydar Nalbantoglu suggests, a postcolonial 'architectural moment' could be captured, "in the immediacy of the present; in the spatial productions of gendered, coloured, historically and psychically constructed bodies; in their engagement with the materiality of space."

It must be emphasised that this particular attitude towards the making of architecture happens in this instance specifically in the context of Sri Lanka, where economic development is not as fast and furious as in the rapidly growing economies of Hong Kong, Singapore, or Taiwan. The architectural production in these countries more often than not in urban centres instead of 'natural' sites. Yet, in recent times, the architecture of Bawa has achieved phenomenal popularity, especially in these cities. This stems from the sheer picturesqueness of his works, which through no fault of Bawa, are so often represented in beautifully shot photographs in magazines and books that their inherent complexities and embeddedness to their contexts become readily reduced to a few attractive images. These intentionally seductive images in turn easily understood and absorbed in their reductive states become readily reproduced in the works of lesser architects. As a result, the proliferation of the Bawa style can be seen in the built landscapes of many Asian cities situated around the tropics, especially in exclusive private residences and holiday beach resorts. The much considered strokes of the Master are reduced to emblematic gestures.

Other Asian architects or architects working in Asia, attempt to address the issues of authenticity and identity differently. Another important figure invoked in one breath with Bawa, is Charles Correa, who introduced the strategy of recalling, adapting still vital Hindu-Indian cultural traditions, in the form of ordering concepts and symbolic systems, to be incorporated as architectural concepts in his version of modern Indian architecture. This particular range of his work is arguably more conceptual, relying on the pre-knowledge of the sources of those ideas. But Correa is more complex than that. Often in his work, other concerns, such as responding to specific climatic conditions, light quality and materiality, congeal into stunningly eidetic images.

Aligned with Correa in the past (the APAC group) with his experiments towards a regional modern architecture, William Lim has since moved on to produce works that manifest his thinking about pluralism in contemporary Asian society. His Marine Parade Community Club featured here, as well as the Robertson Quay Hotel undertaken in collaboration with Tang Guan Bee and Teh Joo Heng, are strong visual statements and formal experiments that have their roots in modern avant gardism where architecture is seen as a form of artistic production and its significance contingent upon its ability to push boundaries, to transgress the normative. Also imbedded in his discourse is an impulse similar to Correa's: to redefine a 'new Asian-ness' manifested as a new Asian architecture, or a new Asian urbanism – and ultimately, a yet to be defined Asian modernity.

The same impulse to ground modern architecture onto the specifics of place and local culture, can be seen in various degrees in the works Rahul Mehrotra, Ernesto Bedmar, Seung H. Sang and Sean Godsell.

For Mehrotra, working primarily in Bombay where the urbanscape is characterised by an intertwining of past and present, the dialogue between specificity of place and universality of an autonomous modern architecture seems a lot more convivial. There is an easy reference to either, not an either/or but an inclusivist attitude that circumvents simple polarisation, to produce always a richly layered work. This attitude allows him to treat all types of work – residences in powerful unified landscapes, interventions in complex urban situations, conservation or preservation projects, with a much freer inventiveness that simultaneously addresses the past, the present and the future.

Bedmar's highly skilled manipulation of form, space, and material – both in architecture and 'landscape' – creates works that are havens of sensuousness. Their specificity to place, in his case defined by him as 'Southeast Asian', is encoded in the dominant use of natural materials and of pitch roofs – for their embodiment of culture specific to this region.

The work of Korean architect, Seung H. Sang, on the other hand, is based on the adaptation of philosophical notions of traditional Korean architectural culture (specifically the Sun Bi spirit or "voluntary restrain") as abstract concepts to the ordering of modern architectural spaces. Such a strategy upholds the ethics of non-excess in contradistinction to the tectonic superfluity of stylistic post-Modernism, yet reveals the potential of a poetic transformation of neutral modern spaces, through an emphasis on the experiential dimension of architecture.

This can be observed too in the work of Sean Godsell, whose architecture with strictly 'Australian' modern roots (with that particular slant towards an identification with the idealised horizontally disposed, dry Australian landscape), clearly wants to locate itself onto the specifics of place, defined in terms topography, materials and light qualities of the site.

Influenced earlier in life by architectural modernism through Le Corbusier, Sert, and former employer Gropius, Tao Ho's later works show a reactionary move away from its generalising effects, that in the need to promote greater 'balance' through diversity, re-exerts his own specificity in clearly ethnic-cultural terms. There is in his work, a conscious dichotomising of 'East' and 'West': the uniformity of 'Western' Modernism countered with a patriotic reference to canonised Chinese cultural heritage. Fundamentally differing from an Eurocentric conception of architecture, his notion of modern architectural production is seen in his wider perspective of history, a history running on cyclical time.

But in Asia right now, this notion of cyclical time is more and more difficult for one to identify with. With the enormous change that is taking contemporary Asia by storm, all identifications built on past cultural traditions and philosophies could all collapse.

Further, today in Asia, the impact of the phenomenon of globalisation is visibly pronounced. In China, hordes of the rural population arrive en masse in the train stations to get a piece of the action in large cities. In Jakarta, Kuala Lumpur, Hong Kong, Taipei, Singapore and Bangkok, the 'MTV' generation has arrived and conspicuously 'hangs out' in shopping malls, before it is time for them to be packed off to universities in the West. Young executives sip café lattes at chic coffee bars; nouveau-riche families spend their weekends scouring condominium show apartments or holiday resort deals. Internet and computer game cafés make their appearances, and transnational unskilled workers take over entire districts on their days off. Through a gentrification process, old quarters in the city and buildings rendered obsolete by the new global economic structure, are thematised and re-adapted for new commercial and cultural uses that the global tourism trade synergetically latches onto. This is the newly configured landscape of Asia.

In rapidly developing economies; land, buildings, construction materials, knowledge, images and space become commodified under the crushing weight of the logic of capital accumulation. Exchange value is all that is left. Traditional values and ideological systems are jettisoned. Could architecture then still be a vital container of identity in our age, where identities are a lot more fluid? And can it still manage to uphold its task under the present phenomenon of extreme increases in built quantities which seems to overwhelm existing strategies of identity, not to mention conventional operative modes of architecture symbolism? Can it survive the onslaught of influences brought about by the incredible electronic revolution? These are the questions the production of architecture in 'new' Asia has to contend with.

In this volume, several voices try to articulate this new landscape in architectural terms. Sometimes, not being too conscious of identity and authenticity can be liberating. Chang Yung Ho's highly conceptual works deal directly with the issue of making architecture in the urban condition of contemporary Chinese cities complicated precisely by this globalised situation. Ideas and concepts for interiors of shops, offices, and so on, are created based on a larger, broader understanding of the contemporary city as it exists now. Instead of relying on the past, Chang finds inspiration and authenticity in the present.

The same can be said about the works of Lim Teng Ngiom (Ngiom Partnership) operating in Malaysia, with his easy identification with contemporary architectural aesthetics, and Nevrat Sayin in Turkey with his easy affiliation with the modern 'hi tech' image.

Tan Kok Meng
EDITOR

The so-called information age is double-edged in that while it habitually inflates the reputation of certain star architects, it nonetheless simultaneously diffuses information on the latest cultural achievements around the world, almost without prejudice, irrespective of the status that may or may not be accorded to so-called regional architects by the critical first world elite. Even so, the spontaneous workings of the media are hardly as transparent or as comprehensive as they might be, so that certain persist and above all our knowledge of the recent architectural production of the Asian world, where with the exception of India, Japan and possibly Australia, we remain ill informed. Even this is overstating the case for while the truly remarkable achievements of the post-war Japanese modern movement are well known, extending up to the present, the rich current production in both South Asia and Australia is still not so familiar outside the confines of these continental expanses, let alone contemporary architectural culture in Singapore, Korea, China and Malaysia, samples of which are featured, however succinctly, in this second volume of Asian Architects, guest edited by Tan Kok Meng. One is particularly gratified to glimpse the hitherto largely unknown work of Seung Hchioh Sang, Ernesto Bedmar, Chang Yung Ho, Lim Teng Ngiom and Tan Kok Meng, for an indication of recent Korean, Chinese, Malaysian and Singapore architecture, along with the recent contributions by more established figures such as Geoffrey Bawa, Charles Correa, William Lim and Tao Ho, in the company of two members of the younger generation in India and Australia respectively, Rahul Mehrotra and Sean Godsell. It is a pleasure to reread Correa's moving excursus on 'open-to-sky' space, particularly as this appears to be realized in his Vidhan Bharan State Assembly, completed in 1996. Here however, apart from the nine-square mandala courtyard plan, the complex is at its most impressive in section and for the way it crowns the profile of the long flat wooded hill on which it sits.

Equally compelling for its topographic section is Rahul Mehrotra's weekend house Shanti, realized outside Alibag in 1997. This is a courtyard house set within a monumental open-to-sky space made out of two parallel basalt stone walls that enclose a civilized zone within a scrub covered, seemingly barren landscape. The back-to-back corrugated iron roofs lifting off the main living spaces, situated north and south of the inner court, harmonize with the contours of distant mountainous landscape while inflecting the horizontal datum established by the bounding walls.

Foreword

One cannot surely claim that this architecture is in anyway figuratively Indian just as one cannot read Ernesto Bedmar's No. 8A Bishopsgate complex as being characteristic of modern Singapore architecture. In fact, both Mehrotra's Shanti House and Bedmar's Bishopsgate House, although quite different in overall area and location, have certain tropes in common, including a central patio and attendant mono-pitched roofs, finished in corrugated sheet in the first instance and ceramic tiles in the second. Cylindrical wooden props and columns also play a prominent role in both houses, by supporting overhanging roofs. However aside from this common vernacular trope, Bedmar has produced a house with Latin American-cum-Wrightian overtones while Mehrotra's house remains unexpectedly evocative of the desert in which it is situated. In fact, it is uncannily evocative in this regard of certain works by the Australian master Glenn Murcutt.

Murcutt brings me by association to Sean Godsell's work at the end of the volume which like a great deal of Australian architecture today is highly sophisticated, bringing one to countenance once again, the refreshing but somehow still surprising fact that one of the most powerful architectural cultures today is, indeed, Australian; a fertile wave in fact, borne forward here by Godsell's Kew House, Melbourne (1997) and his St. Paul's School Art Faculty, completed one year later. Both works seem are of the greatest delicacy, in terms of siting, spatial organization and material, a synthesis which is succinctly summed up as a generic sensibility by Godsell himself:

Although apparently 'modern' in its language, the house is primordial in its intent *en rust*, oiled second-hand boards, recycled decking and a lack of ëprecious detail combine with rudimentary services to form a house which is elemental rather than processed. Operable steel shutters shade the north and west elevations. A passive evaporative cooling system takes the prevailing southwesterly wind over the grass embankment and under the house where it is introduced via floor vents to the east end of the building. The air is further cooled by fine water mist sprays placed at the top end of the embankment.

In certain respects Godsell's work is not so far removed from the sensibility of the Sri Lankan old school gentleman-architect Geoffrey Bawa, although they could not be further apart in terms of age, background and know-how. Be this as it may, one of the most beautiful and mysterious works by Bawa that is touched on all too briefly here is his tile roofed Madurai Club in India, about which he laconically informs the reader that it was largely conceived by the stone masons who built it with a little encouragement from the architect.

Surely one of the most intellectual and challenging contributions to this volume is the work of the young Chinese architect, Chang Yung Ho, who has obviously been exposed to the minimalist mannerism of Japanese architects Hiromi Fujii, Toyo Ito and Kasuo Shinohara although there are aspects of his architecture that suggest brief encounters with Peter Eisenman or even Diener and Diener. This said, there is something subversively ideogrammatic, not to say terroristic, about his architecture. Thus his bookstores in Nanchang and Beijing appear as labyrinthic commentaries on the congested combative character of Chinese metropolitan life, thereby bringing the browser to re-experience, amid closely packed book-stacks, mobile or fixed, all the alienating, frustrating, yet at times seductive confrontations with big city life. Chang Yung Ho's intellectual irony is played out, in an altogether more complex way in his Vertical Den City or Upside Down Office, realized for Cummins Asia in Beijing in 1997. Here we are witness to a cinematic game with headless bodies that transforms the panoptic ambulatory experience of the typical office corridor into a mysterious translucent labyrinth while the private office becomes a voyeuristic underworld where one can see nothing except feet, the framings plates of all but frameless obscured

From Where I'm Standing: A Virtual View

glass running from desk top height to the ceiling. This oscillation between revealing and concealing is enriched by unexpected perspectival recessions and reflections ricocheting back and forth across the space.

Such intellectuality is quite removed from Lim Teng Ngiom's new Malaysian architecture where latter-day European Purism, filtered through the work of OMA, surfaces with refreshing energy and sculptural authority, within a Malaysian context. Surely there is as much of Rem Koolhaas as there is of Le Corbusier in the PKLC building in Port Klang or the Wisma Laju building or even in the less audacious Pat's House dating from 1999, where the architect lays out a work which is as unequivocally Asian as it is uncompromisingly modern in its calm display of dynamic horizontal form. What is it that is Malaysian here one asks oneself? Is it the canted walls, vaguely reminiscent of some local vernacular, or is it the systematically gridded curtain walling under the mono-pitched roofs? Or is it the detached, rigid jalousies suspended from the cantilevered downstand beams of square cruciform columns, or finally, is it the exposed reinforced concrete frame itself with its dynamic canted props that sustain the cantilevered terrace and living room as they slide off the gentle hillside slope into the blue?

This resume would totally fail as a comprehensive overview were I not to mention the remarkably sophisticated criticism pieces by Gülsüm Baydar Nalbantoglu and Paul Carter, two essays that challenge, in different but at times uncannily similar ways, our received views of the post-colonial predicament in our global internet age. What remains unclear in both of these pieces is how architecture *in se* relates in any way to either the old or the new cultural strategies of resistance, repudiation and renewal, particularly where these positions are predicated on discourses that are quintessentially sculptural or theatrical and hence not in essence architectural at all?

Kenneth Frampton

1994 saw the first English edition of Hanno-Walter Kruft's monumental work: *A History of Architectural Theory: From Virtruvius to the Present*.[1] It is an important survey as much for its exclusions as its inclusions for anyone who is interested in architecture. The title reiterates a number of familiar themes. Vitruvius is the founding father of architectural theory; there is a linear development of architectural theory from Vitruvius to the present; and the domain of architectural theory is the Western world. Indeed as the table of contents clearly indicates, the geographical span of the survey is limited to the European continent and the United States with one section on the Soviet Union. A history of Western architectural theory then, unabashedly presents itself as a history of architectural theory. But really, has there been architectural theory outside the West? If, as Kruft contends, architectural theory is constituted by architectural discourse, has there been such discourse outside the West? Indeed, has there been architecture outside the West? These are large questions that should not be answered too quickly with blind commitment to some form of political correctness.

"What is architecture?" is a tired question repeatedly asked by theorists of the discipline. It indicates the desire to carve a space for "architecture" from an indecipherable plenitude that includes "non-architecture." This is simultaneously a desire to delineate boundaries, to control the disciplinary terms of reference, and to retain the authority to judge. Some of the fundamental categories of the architectural discipline, such as architecture/building, high-style/vernacular, modern/primitive, and Western/non-Western are based precisely on this necessity. The crucial historical moment that remains unattended in Kruft's survey, i.e., the moment of colonial encounters, plays a significant role in these demarcations. The first term of each pair unquestionably falls into the accepted parameters of the architectural discipline. The status of the second terms, on the other hand, has been a continuous burden on it. These are neither entirely outside nor totally inside architecture's disciplinary boundaries. Architectural discourse needs them but needs to keep them at bay. But which architectural discourse are we talking about here? To answer that, I need to turn to the Virtruvian heritage, which established the primacy of vision, the autonomy of architectural form and the linear history of the master subject as the foundational myths of the discipline.[2] This heritage is important to remember for the unequal architectural encounter between the coloniser and the colonised, the lineage of Western architectural theory governs the limit for all possible architectural identifications. Psychoanalytical theory reminds us that any identity depends upon "the other" for its confirmation as well as for the expression of its meaning and desires. Constituting categories of "the other" for the architectural discipline proper, the second terms of the binary pairs fulfil precisely that function.

Let me now dwell upon the primal scene when Western architecture encountered, and cast its gaze on, its non-Western other. That is the historical moment not only when Western architecture identifies itself as such but also when non-Western architectural scenes were placed in the position of being-looked-at. I use the term gaze in the Lacanian sense here. "In the scopic regime," contends Jacques Lacan, "the gaze is outside, I am looked at, that is to say, I am a picture. ...What determines me, at the most profound level, in the visible, is the gaze that is outside."[3] In his model, from the moment the subject is looked at, s/he tries to adapt to the gaze. The gaze is everywhere and nowhere. It is apprehended more by its effects than by its source. I would argue that the canonical premises of the architectural discipline function similarly and constitute the architectural gaze. Hence, when a certain body of knowledge, which had identified and established itself as "architecture" in the Western world prior to colonisation, encountered another, the two terms, "architecture" and "the West," coalesced in unprecedented ways. At one level, the encounter between the West and its outside is also an encounter between architecture and its outside; in other words, between architecture and what had yet not been named as such. The story of architecture becomes the story of identity and difference between unequal partners in an unprecedented relationship. The architectural scene is complicated with new terms of reference for both sides of the new division.

1 Translated by R. Taylor, E. Callander and A. Wood, Princeton Architectural Press, New York, 1994. The book first appeared in 1985 under the title, *Geschichte der Architekturtheorie: Von der Antike bis zur Gegenwart.*
2 For a thorough analysis of the architectural canon in these terms see Mirjana Lozanovska, *Excess: A Thesis on (Sexual) Difference and Architecture*, unpublished Ph.D. Thesis, Deakin University, Melbourne, 1994, especially chapter 1.
3 Jacques Lacan, *The Four Concepts of Psychoanalysis*, W.W. Norton, New York, 1981, p. 106. I have largely benefited from Kaja Silverman's explanation of this notion in *The Threshold of the Visible World*, Routledge, New York, 1996.

Gülsüm Baydar Nalbantoglu

(Post) Colonial Architectural Encounters

Fig. 1 Sir Banister Fletcher's illustration of Indian Saracenic details. Sir Banister Fletcher, *A History of Architecture on the Comparative Method for the Student Craftsman, and Amateur*, B. T. Batsford Ltd., London, 1954, sixteenth ed., p. 959.

Fig. 2 Bernard Rudofsky's exhibition, *Architecture Without Architects* at the New York Museum of Modern Art in 1964. Bernard Rudofsky, *The Prodigious Builders*, Harvest, New York, 1977, p. 367.

First scene: Writing history

Monumental architectural statements of the colonists were unfamiliar spectacles for Western architects. From Fischer von Erlach to Sir Banister Fletcher and others, post eighteenth century architectural discourse is inscribed by accounts of Western architecture's encounters with other architecture. The problem, of course, is how to describe, define and understand architectural traditions that may be radically different from what had been known as architecture and what had been given-to-be-seen by the architectural discipline until then. The given boundaries of architecture are threatened.

One of the primary figures of the Virtruvian heritage, Leon Batista Alberti, had taught Western architects that beauty refers to the "harmony of all parts, in whatsoever subject it appears, fitted together with such proportion and connection, that nothing could be added, diminished or altered, but for the worse."[4] It is not surprising then, that equipped with this knowledge, the Western gaze diagnosed both surplus and lack in non-Western architectural cultures. Something was taken away and something was added in excess. Fletcher's *A History of Architecture on the Comparative Method for the Student Craftsman, and Amateur* conveys this point with impeccable clarity. Until 1901, the book was a modest survey of European styles. After then, it was considerably enlarged to include Indian, Chinese, Japanese, Central American and Saracenic architectural cultures as well. Fletcher curiously gathers the latter under a section entitled, "non-historical styles." The prefix "non" signifies a lack. Fletcher explains:[5]

> These non-historical styles can scarcely be as interesting from an architect's point of view as those of Europe, which have progressed by the successive solution of construction problems, resolutely met and overcome; for in the East decorative schemes seem generally to have overweighed all other considerations."

Fletcher's detailed account of non-historical styles is marked simultaneously by a fascination and an apparent unease with the overuse of ornamentation in non-Western architectural cultures. His descriptions are loaded not only with such terms as "bewildering richness" and "majestic beauty," but also with derogatory terms like "bizarre," "striving after excess" and "grotesque."[6] According to Fletcher, styles that lack history are marked with ornamental excess. (fig. 1)

Lack and excess are terms that are theorised in disciplines other than architecture. Following these I would argue that in Fletcher's discourse, lack serves for Western architecture's attributes to be oppositionally articulated; excess renders it adequate to the coloniser's desire.[7] European styles were qualified as "historical" only when an oppositional relationship with non-European styles appeared on the agenda. Western architecture had to redefine its identity in positive terms in relation to another that lacked positivity. In other words, the label "historical styles," becomes possible only after the naming of non-Western styles as non-historical. The attribution of lack to the other serves to positively

4 Leone Batisti Alberti, *The Ten Books of Architecture*, reprint of the 1755 Leoni edition, Dover Publications, New York, 1986, p .113.
5 Sir Banister Fletcher, *A History of Architecture on the Comparative Method for the Student Craftsman, and Amateur*, B. T. Batsford Ltd., London, 1954, sixteenth edition, p. 888.
6 *Ibid.*, pp. 888, 893, 961. I have argued elsewhere that Fletcher's text can be read in other ways to suggest the recognition of radical alterity in non-Western architectural cultures. Here I want to emphasise his explicit references to notions of lack and excess. See my "Towards Postcolonial Openings: Re-reading Sir Banister Fletcher's *History of Architecture*," in Assemblage 35.
7 Here I reproduce Kaja Silverman's explanation of lack and plenitude in terms of the identification of the female subject. See *The Threshold of the Visible World*, Routledge, New York, 1996, p. 33.

Fig. 3 Sudanese cliff dwellings as photographed by Bernard Rudofsky. Bernard Rudofsky, *Architecture Without Architects: A Short Introduction to Non-pedigreed Architecture*, Doubleday, New York, 1964, p. 40-41.

Fig. 4 Advertisement for Hilton Batang Ai Resort, Sarawak. *The Straits Times*, Singapore, April 30, 1997, p. 22.

identify the self. In Fletcher's discourse, the lack of historicity is complemented with an excess of ornamentation. What is noted as excess in the other, is also the cause of pleasure as its extravagance covers over the lack.

Fletcher, of course, does not dwell upon such notions in his book. He quickly dispenses with his momentary pleasure by submitting non-Western architecture under the same framework of analysis as the rest. The comparative method that he had established in the first edition pervades the succeeding ones. The line drawings that depict the "excessive" ornamentation in "non-historical styles" are identical in technique to the rest. The other enters the domain of architecture in terms that have already been established prior to its appearance. Yet the source of Fletcher's jouissance lies in the excess that architecture-as-he-knows is unable to represent. The architectural gaze that is cast over Fletcher's look to the non-Western scene enables him simultaneously to recognise and to cover his momentary pleasure.

Second Scene: Writing architecture

The nineteenth century of colonial architectural gaze turned to the non-West for its monumental gestures, i.e., palaces, temples and mosques. The postcolonial world – and I use the term in a strictly chronological sense here – witnessed a significant shift in interest. An important turning point came in 1964, with the opening of an exhibition at the New York Museum of Modern Art. Entitled, "Architecture Without Architects," the exhibition contained over 150 photographs of anonymous buildings and settings taken by architect Bernard Rudofsky. (fig. 2) These ranged from Capadoccian carved dwellings to bamboo pole structures in the Gulf of New Guinea. The exhibition was staged in the manner of an architectural manifesto. Rudofsky was critical of Western architecture's concern with "a few select cultures... a small part of the globe... a who's who of architects who commemorated power and wealth, and an anthology of buildings of, by and for the privileged."[8]

Through Rudofsky's exemplary effort, the audience of the Museum of Modern Art was introduced to the other half of the built environment untouched by the master architect's intervention. It is difficult to disagree with Rudofsky's reaction against this aspect of the architectural canon. In his haste to correct this "error", however, Rudofsky overlooks the fact that the canon is also based on the privileging of the visual, notions of origin and progress and a binary system of thinking. For Rudofsky's system, too, is structured around the binary opposites of high-style/vernacular; authored/anonymous; individual/communal; the "architectural blight in industrial countries" versus the "serenity of the architecture in so-called underdeveloped countries." The powerful black and white images in "Architecture Without Architects" display intricately sculpted buildings and settlements, which merge comfortably into their natural settings.

8 Bernard Rudofsky, *Architecture Without Architects: A Short Introduction to Non-pedigreed Architecture*, Doubleday, New York, 1964, p. 1.

Fig. 5 SOM and Sedad Eldem, Hilton Hotel, Istanbul, 1952. Renata Holod and Ahmet Evin, eds., *Modern Turkish Architecture,* University of Pennsylvania Press, Philadelphia, 1984, p. 109.

Rudofsky's characteristically humanist approach enables him to homogenise local architectural traditions based on the naturalistic essence. In this architectural narrative, Spanish streets (80) and Syrian water wheels (106), Anatolian carved dwellings and African granaries exist side by side, all set against the notion of insensitive, commercialised and industrialised qualities of a generalised notion of "Western" architecture. The photo captions emphasise sculptural and aesthetic qualities, permanence, exceptional imagination and artistic insight. Rudofsky's agenda becomes clear when he states that

> The present exhibition is the vehicle of the idea that the philosophy and know-how of the anonymous builders presents the largest untapped source of architectural inspiration for industrial man.[9]

Rudofsky's heroic project, then, makes him the living agent and witness for otherwise lost architectural traditions. But lost to whom? At one important level, his enterprise is but one instance whereby a narrative of local traditions serves as a critique of Western architecture's self-made trajectory. Rudofsky's oppositional narrative originates from Western architecture's founding principles based on the aura of the autonomous architectural object. The vernacular is named and transformed, through the architectural gaze, into a standing reserve for the pleasure of the architect. Architecture without architects, i.e., architecture that lacks architects, is now included in the grand narrative of architecture with architects. The two terms that structured Fletcher's discourse, lack and excess, can be read differently in Rudofsky's narrative. This time it is Western architecture that lacks the wisdom of anonymous builders and is in excess of industrialisation. In a manner that is strikingly different from Fletcher's, Rudofsky's source of pleasure, too, is rooted in what he identifies as excess, i.e., his camera – a product of Western industrial technology. For it is his dramatically shot black and white images that render architecture without architects desirable to the architectural audience. Let me illustrate.

In one striking instance in "Architecture Without Architects", facing pages show two views of a Sudanese tribal settlement: A bird's eye-view and a close-up. (fig.3) "What at first glance appears to be mere debris," Rudofsky discloses, houses a "highly sophisticated culture" known to produce some of the best examples of African art.[10] The eye of the camera illuminates the tribal settlement in the manner of a projector. In doing so it explicates secrets, restores identities and corrects mistakes. In both cases the illumination that lights up the tribal settlement has its origins elsewhere. The camera's double-move removes the viewer twice from the tribal settlement. Rudofsky literally shows possible ways of seeing it. His first shot shows what the Sudanese settlement is not, i.e., non-architecture. The second one shows what it is, i.e., architecture. Rudofsky's look enables him to project a different image on the screen of the same object that the gaze had denied architectural status. His camera enables him to return life (architecture) to the dead (debris).

But does it?

9 Rudofsky, p. 7.
10 Rudofsky, p. 40-41.

Fig. 6   The Rock Garden, Chandigarh, wall texture.

Fig. 7   The Rock Garden, Chandigarh, figurines.

I would argue that the architectural gaze that is cast over Rudofsky's camera participates in a double-murder – double death. The Sudanese tribal settlement is killed once by analogy to debris and once more by analogy to architecture. Both Roland Barthes and Kaja Silverman dwell on death in relation to photography. Barthes contends that photography transforms subjects into objects. Being photographed, he says, one is neither subject nor object, but a subject who feels s/he is becoming an object. The moment of becoming a spectre, to him, is an experience of a micro-version of death. Silverman, on the other hand, argues that both the camera and the gaze confer a spectacular body on the subject, which concurs with the death of its existential body. I do not suggest, of course, that the Sudanese tribal settlement is marked by an essential identity, which is murdered by the architect's camera. Each such recording, far from recording, far from destroying or capturing an architectural essence, inscribes another layer of meaning on the site/building that is frozen by the camera. Rather than bestowing immortality, architectural recording marks the death of buildings. It affirms architecture through death. Yet such records are necessary to confer architectural identity upon any building. It is through these that buildings are recognised as architecture. The inclusion then, of a Sudanese tribal settlement into the category of architecture involves a violent act of exclusion. Both the category of architecture and Sudanese tribal settlement are thus deprived of other possible interpretations and identifications that might have proliferated from the encounter between architecture and its outside, architecture and non-architecture.

Rudofsky is clearly capable of seeing other than what is given-to-be-seen. Yet his look is governed by the imperative to return to those images that provide fantasmatic origins for his own imaginary identification. Architecture without architects, then, provides a substitute to architectural desires that are repressed by the architectural discipline.

Third scene: Writing back?

So far I have looked at only one side of the screen that separates the coloniser from the colonised. What happens on the other side, i.e., that of the colonised? The moment it is seen, the architecture of the colonised is held to an involuntary identification. It is named, analysed, described, drawn and photographed. In relation to being photographed Roland Barthes says that:[11]

> Now, once I feel myself observed by the lens, everything changes: I constitute myself in the process of "posing". I instantaneously make another body for myself, I transform myself in advance into an image... but... "myself" never coincides with my image; for it is the image which is heavy, motionless, stubborn (which is why society sustains it), and "myself" which is light, divided, dispersed.

11 Roland Barthes, *Camera Lucida*, trans. Richard Howard, Fontana paperbacks, London, 1984, pp. 10, 12.

The issue here is the primal scene when the other feels/knows that s/he is being looked-at; that s/he is the object of the gaze that makes him/her a spectacle. The key terms that define non-Western architecture; i.e., "non-West" and "architecture", are loaded with a-priori significance. The "non" of the non-West can be read parallel to Fletcher's "non" of the non-historical. Non-Western architecture is an identification that restructures both sides of the equation between the West and the non-West and architecture and non-architecture. I would argue that these two discourses, exemplified by Fletcher and Rudofsky, have organised this equation. The familiar binary pairs, Western and regional, international and national, global and local, overlap with another set of pairs consisting of disciplinary terms such as architecture and building, high-style and vernacular, modern and primitive. If Fletcher privileges and idealises one side of the equation, Rudofsky does the opposite. The terms of the equation are kept intact in both cases.

A non-Western essence that is implicated in the term non-Western architecture, (whether despised or idealised for these are two sides of the same coin) disappears the moment it is named as such. For it is already named in other terms, terms that are possible only in relation to already established categories. I would argue that the cultural identity of architects who design and build outside the West hardly matter in this scenario. Architectural discourses of decolonised cultures have conveniently adapted the familiar binary pairs of the discipline. International versus national/regional are the most prevalent terms in these contexts. In many instances, while international Modernism becomes the symbol of progress, architectural regionalism appears as the formal expression of cultural nationalism. Architecture aligns with nationalist agendas and state policies. It claims nation-based roots and contained territory. In other cases the architectural interest in the local and the regional takes on commercial value. In architectural critic Kenneth Frampton's terms, architectural codes turn into "consumerist iconography masquerading as culture." If masquerade means making a show of what one is not, it is a powerful term to describe the architectural identifications of decolonised cultures so far as these are sought through the representational parameters of another's image.

The issue becomes increasingly pertinent as decolonisation enables new forms of transnational and transcultural architectural movements aided by the growth of the global market for architecture. Familiar terms are realigned in unprecedented ways. Different histories, temporalities, nationalities and languages are brought into contact at a global scale. The formerly colonised part of the world obviously has a different relationship to the architectural scene than before. Yet the concepts of traditional, regional and local are persistently re-cited in architectural discourse and practice.

Let me now turn to a recent example.

In 1995 Hilton International Batang Ai Longhouse Resort in Malaysia won an award of distinction as the best tourist attraction in ASEAN.[12] The resort boasts of offering unique opportunities to be close to nature without having to depart from modern living. Its full-page newspaper advertisement includes a bird's eye view. (fig. 4) I am struck by the way that the buildings that mimic the indigenous long houses of Sarawak turn away from the lake and embrace a swimming pool. The design is by Kumpulan Parabena, a Malaysian architectural firm. Then I remember another architectural encounter with Hilton during my architectural education in Turkey. For in texts on contemporary Turkish architecture, the Istanbul Hilton Hotel of 1952, designed by leading American architectural firm SOM (Skidmore, Owings and Merrill) and a Turkish architect Sedad Eldem, is introduced as an early landmark of "International Style" architecture in Turkey. My book on modern Turkish architecture explains that "elements of traditional architecture were incorporated into the arcaded shopping complex and into the shell-like structure of the nightclub."[13] (fig. 5) These are signature elements of the "native" architectural partner who is well known for his detailed study of traditional Turkish architecture. In black and white image, I can spot the nightclub structure with difficulty as is dwarfed by the scale of the "modern" hotel.

Hence the name Hilton calls forth an unlikely conjunction of names from the field of architecture: Anonymous builders of Sarawak longhouses, Kumpulan Parabena, SOM, Sedad Eldem; Malaysia, Istanbul and North America. If it is relatively easy to distinguish between the "international-modern" and "regional" components of the Istanbul Hilton; that is not the case in the Batang Ai Longhouse Resort. At first sight, the repressed architectural signifiers of the second term of modern/traditional and international/regional pairs seem to have taken the dominant role in Sarawak. By all "architectural" standards, Batang Ai Longhouse Resort privileges building over architecture, tradition over modern, local over international. Yet it is designed by a proper architectural firm commissioned by an international hotel chain for global tourists whose retreat is organised around the familiar blue mosaics of a swimming pool. Immaculate architectural scripts, which separated architecture from building, international from local, modern from traditional, and which associated the first term with the West and the second with the rest, are seemingly threatened.

But are they really? Is there really an architectural difference between the modernist gesture of SOM in Istanbul and the regionalist gesture of Kumpulan Parabena? Perhaps globalisation is a term that covers over architectural repressions that have little to do with geographical identities. Whether internationally, nationally or culturally based, architectural identifications are powerful tools. In the speedy development of global markets such titles as "Tropical Architecture" and "Asian House" proliferate in the cosmopolitan centres. The first terms indicate different cultural identities. Yet they depend on the second term, architecture, which remains unquestioned. For the image of architecture is already constituted prior to the emergence of tropical, Asian, Indian or Chinese architectures. Hence such identifications are not only essentialist constructs, but also such essentialism entails an a-priori construction "outside" the identification in question.

12 *The Straits Times*, Singapore, April 30, 1997, p. 22, advertisement.
13 Renata Holod and Ahmet Evin, eds., *Modern Turkish Architecture*, University of Pennsylvania Press, Philadelphia, 1984, p. 110.

Fourth scene: Un-writing history, un-writing architecture

Are there possibilities of identification for (non-Western) architectures other than their idealised image? Can we conceive of non-Western architecture, non-architecture as neither surplus nor lack? Can we attribute a productive plenitude rather than lack to the prefix "non"? To what extent is it possible to undo the architectural gaze? Is there any way to look at architecture differently?

I have used the notion of the gaze in describing the hold of the canonised principles of the architectural discipline across different localities and cultures. Silverman, following Lacan, explains that the look is different from and independent of the gaze.[14] If the gaze is a mechanism, almost a power devoid of subjectivity, she says, the look is always embodied and hence inscribed by temporality and desire. Silverman insists that the look is an active agent, which is capable of seeing other than what is given-to-be-seen. Therein lie its productive and creative capacities. For an architectural instance of the productive look I want to return to the themes of waste and excess on which I dwelled in the case of the Sudanese tribal settlement.

My site now is a public garden, known as the Rock Garden, in Chandigarh, India. Located in a former site of industrial waste, it is the labourious product of a road inspector, Sh. Nek Chand. The Rock Garden is literally made of waste: pots, bottles, broken objects and all kinds of ceramic, metal and plastic trash. Its labyrinthine experience provides fantasmatic paths of discovery. Unusual objects, textures and surfaces bring about magical experiences.[15] (fig. 6) Pieces of broken plates, spare parts of sanitary appliances and defective earthenware are transformed almost beyond recognition. The garden has its permanent inhabitants in the form of numerous figurines, both human and animal. Made of waste as well, and conspicuously genderless, these figurines are situated in miniature communities, dancing, greeting their viewers or just standing in peace. (fig. 7) They are silent witnesses of the possibility of seeing beauty in debris, life in death. Permanence and immortality – obsessions of the architectural discipline – take on a different meaning in the Rock Garden. Here, rather than belonging to a finished form, the notion of permanence points to a continuing process of translations and transformations. The Rock Garden flees from architecture's structuring reflection of cities, buildings and open spaces. It bears testimony to the possibility of looking differently, seeing other than what is given to be seen. As such, it marks an instance of fertility and procreation rather than a statement of frozen architectural truths.

In the Rock Garden, Rudofsky's statement that the philosophy and know-how of anonymous builders present the largest untapped source of architectural inspiration for industrial man is turned upside down. Here it is industry itself that has presented an untapped source of architectural inspiration for the local builder. Not only the proper categories architecture but also those of industrial production are effectively undermined. The Rock Garden opens up a series of issues on the role locality in architecture

14 Silverman, *Threshold*, especially p. 180-185.
15 At one level my own photographic representations of the Rock Garden bear the burden of architectural representation that I argue in this paper. I must emphasise that they are not meant to construct a finite architectural reality but should be seen as what they are: photographic representations of partial scenes from a garden.

beyond regional(ist) and national(ist) constructs. Here locality does not address any notion of cultural identity. There are no mandalas, no trace of "Indianness" as architectural convention would like to see, but an engagement with the immediacy of a given set of circumstances. Located in close proximity to Le Corbusier's parliamentary complex, the Rock Garden does not participate in a complementary or oppositional gesture. It is a silent interruption to the grand narrative of the masters – a silent refusal to participate. The Rock Garden is a postcolonial gesture to the extent that it effectively undermines the categorical imperatives of the architectural gaze in relation to non-Western architectures.

If the entire discourse on local and regional buildings is one that comes to us constructed by an always already defined notion of architecture, the question, I would argue, is not how to include these in architectural discourse but to see how other architectures disrupt the given categories of architectural discourse. Once conceptualised as a signification rather than a finite disciplinary field, architecture can be productively dismantled. Postcolonial "architectural moments" can then be captured in the immediacy of the present; in their engagement with the materiality of space. I am thinking of architectural discourses that are neither universalist nor particularist but which engage with the concrete historical circumstances that produce different modes of architecture and spatiality. Thinking postcoloniality in architecture then does not merely entail an engagement with previously colonised cultures; it is but one of the many practices which make it possible to engage with boundaries which guard architecture's cultural and disciplinary presuppositions; boundaries which remain intact through exclusionary practices that remain unquestioned once the institutional structure of the discipline is established. Thinking postcoloniality in architecture questions architecture's intolerance to difference, to the unthought, to its outside. For it embraces the premise that "difference, like authenticity, is produced not salvaged."[16]

On a final note, if I return to the title of Kruft's book, *A History of Architectural Theory: From Virtruvius to the Present*, I may read something else in it than I initially suggested. Placing the emphasis on the first word, I am tempted to see the book humbly presenting itself as "a" history of architectural theory which implies that there are other possible histories, other ways of constituting architectural history, and perhaps even architecture itself.

16 Trinh H. Minh Ha, "Of Other Peoples: Beyond the 'Salvage Paradigm'" in Hal Foster, ed., *Discussions in Contemporary Culture* (Seattle: Bay Press, 1987), p. 140.

Origin,
although a
historical
category,
has,
nevertheless,
nothing in
common with
emergence.

Walter Benjamin[1]

Paul Carter ___

| To Let The Wind Through |

architecture, heritage, performance

1 Eduardo Cadava, *Words of Light*, Princeton University Press: Princeton, New Jersey, 1997, p.19.
2 Tao Ho, 'Energy, Environment, and Heritage: The Need for a Paradigm Shift' in *Anywise*, edited by Cynthia C. Davidson, MIT Press: Cambridge, Mass, 1996, p.78.

From the top: International Style
skyline, Bangkok, view from Mung
Tun Thani by Nation Fender, 1995;
Tao Ho, AJ Universal Center, Suzhou;
Tao Ho, Mt. Qing Long Spa and
Vacation Houses, West Lake,
Hangzhou.

Perhaps nowhere are issues of heritage more keenly discussed than in the ex-colonial nations of South-East Asia. Rapid population growth, modernisation and urbanisation combine to transform the human and physical landscape. Not only old buildings but old belief systems, indigenous languages and even the familiar topography are swept away by the bulldozers of economic rationalism. Architects, if they have any conscience, find themselves in an odd position: colluding in the massive destruction of the vernacular built fabric, they appropriate its stylistic hallmarks to lend their late-Modernist frames a local identity. Positioning the local as exotic, they build the appearance of the new city on a colossal disappearance act. This at least was the charge levelled against Hong Kong-based architect Tao Ho's Suzshou and Hangzhou projects at the 1995 *Anywise* conference held in Seoul.

At the conference Ho himself had been critical of Western-style urbanisation which, as the symbol of rapid national development, encourages the public to view their historic buildings "as reminders of a backwardness that they would prefer to forget." Ho had enthusiastically advocated traditional building practices and forms; he had expressed a sharp distaste for post-modern eclecticism – an understandable reaction to the characterless International Style, but resulting in "building caricatures of history." Finally, Ho had expressed his own ambition for "a harmonious dialogue with nature, heritage, and technology... Our task is to reassemble the isolated parts of our world and form a holistic picture."[2] Nothing objectionable in this, one would have thought, especially in the West where the language of interactivity and multidisciplinearity has been in circulation for the last thirty years.

What, then, was the problem? Why did the European architects dismiss Tao Ho's Hangzhou development – a vacation village and health spa on top of a hill with a view of West Lake which, Ho explained, was inspired by "the picturesque description of a lost village found in a poem from the Tang Dynasty... I want people to see it as a recreation of a lost village [and] to achieve this, I must allow local heritage, building forms, materials, colour, and texture to prevail – as "a 'joke', 'a caricature' and 'inauthentic'." Why did architect Peter Eisenman find Tao Ho's Suzhou commercial shopping centre, "situated in the most sensitive part of the ancient city", so much kitsch?[3]

Partly it could be explained as cultural illiteracy. This at least was Tao Ho's view. European architects of a Modernist persuasion are hung up, he thought, on a Platonic idea of architectural form: they think the only authentic design is one that is internally, formally harmonious. But it is this *tabula rasa* mentality, this indifference to the local and the vernacular, that has produced our characterless late 20th century conurbations. Partly, too, Westerners, preoccupied with a return to authentic origins, cannot grasp the incremental character of Chinese tradition, evolutionary rather than revolutionary.

But partly, I think, the disagreement reflected a deeper crisis – a recognition on the part of all parties that "cultural heritage" and "architectural form" could no longer be assumed to be synonymous. The fact is that, in appealing to heritage values, architects admit to the groundlessness, the historical detachment, of their practices: Tao Ho was ironically right when he described an intention to recreate *what had never existed*. This is what perturbed the Europeans: in his frank admission they recognised the unsustainability of their own position. What is the difference between the ideal village of the European tradition and Ho's lost village? They are alike architectural utopias.

The Spanish architectural theorist, Ignasi de Solà-Morales suggests that we have reached a point where "Traditional architectural instruments of analysis scarcely engage or have the capacity to respond to [the] constituent parts of the life of the metropolis – transportation networks, highways, spaces reserved for the logistics of distribution, protected natural areas, virtual spaces for communication and entertainment."[4] His point can be applied to the life of the past in the modern city: architecturally based approaches to the preservation of historic buildings (leaving aside the fact that these offer a very narrow definition of cultural heritage) are unable to respond to the "constituent parts" lending these sites their social significance. What, to continue with Solà-Morales' analogy, can a respect for building forms, materials, textures and colours tell us about buildings as structures of movement, as performative spaces, or as designs for communication?

3 Tao Ho, echoing comments of Rem Koolhaas in *Anywise*, p.115.
4 Ignasi de Solà-Morales, 'Present and Futures, Architecture in Cities in *Thresholds*, MIT Press, Cambridge, Mass, 1997, issue 14, p.18.

5   Kisho Kurokawa, *Intercultural Architecture, the philosophy of symbiosis*, Academy Editions, London, 1991, p.179.
6   Kisho Kurokawa, *Intercultural Architecture, the philosophy of symbiosis*, p.180.

An emphasis on historic sites as informational structures helps us, incidentally, to resolve the stand-off between Ho and his critics. Both parties seemed to regard architecture *theatrically*, as a container existing apart from the social, economic and political life it generates; despite Ho's appeal to interconnectedness, there is no sense that architecture might be (and Sola-Morales implies should be) a branch of cybernetics, that is, understood as an important medium of communication. In a sense it doesn't matter what Hanzhou village represents, whether it is historically accurate or postmodern kitsch. In a globalised economy where cultural heritage, cultural tourism and development lobbies strategically borrow one another's vocabulary to advance their interests, what matters is the new design's capacity to operate effectively as part of an information network. It is as a vector, as an agent of movement and exchange, that it is to be valued – in its capacity to bring into circulation the *image* of a lost village, and hence to bring into symbiosis "restoration" and "redevelopment."

These last terms come from Japanese architect, Kisho Kurokawa who, like Tao Ho, is an outspoken critic of Western rationalism and its architectural incarnation, Modernism. Unlike Ho, however, Kurokawa understands cultural heritage strategically, as a key player in developing viable regional redevelopment policies. To design truly functional urban-infrastructure – to meet Solà-Morales' criticism that architecture fails to intervene in the "life" of the city – it must, Kurokawa argues, acknowledge the mobility that characterises modern society: "in our information society, mobility has begun to possess considerable value for its own sake," and he proposes in the Japanese context that "Cities will be connected by transportation and information networks that will weave a spider's web of linked cities, in a symbiosis of centralisation and decentralisation."[5]

Here the role of cultural heritage is clear: it is to promote economic activity. To meet the demand of the new consumer – a species Kurokawa dubs *homo movens* – cities must provide a wealth of choices. It is clearly uneconomic to replicate these choices in every city. Therefore cities must divide the choices regionally, one promoting its Kabuki theatre, another its operas, in this way creating a network of opportunities. To underpin such initiatives, an "event economy" needs to be planned, a calendar of local events which generates income by attracting visitors from outside the region. As an example of what he has in mind Kurokawa cites the governor of Oita Prefecture, who "has led a successful 'village product' campaign, in which many events have been held."[6]

This is the true meaning of Tao Ho's "lost village" concept: the creation of an idea which, in the name of cultural heritage, encourages local investment. His *navet* (in his critics' view) was to speak in terms of a heritage of architectural forms, as if he took a *critical* stance towards present-day trends in commercial building developments. The motivation of his design was not archaeological curiosity about the past, not a desire to preserve living traditions, but simply a pragmatic necessity to insert his development successfully into an economy of competing signs, to create a brand name that attracted consumption.

Tao Ho's village succeeds if it becomes a medium for communication and entertainment. In this sense it is no different from an office, an airport or indeed the governor's "village." The Europeans objected to this because of their belief in architecture's critical responsibility to examine its own foundations, to revisit its own origins. Ho, by contrast, felt no need to undertake this enquiry. Not accepting the Western split between man and nature, and rejoicing in the continuity of the Chinese tradition, he saw his task as one of reparation, restoration and redevelopment going hand in hand. In any case as Ole Bouman commented, observing the utter inability of Western and Asian (the term was symptomatic of the lingering imperialism present) architects to address each other at the Seoul meeting, The entire Western preoccupation with the impossibility of any true foundation, in stone and in thought, is here set aside.[7]

This brief discussion of the issues raised by Tao Ho's projects underlines the point that cultural heritage has different definitions in different cultures. Nor should this be interpreted simply as an East-West divide. Criticising Yanagi Souetsu's efforts to prevent the occupying Japanese government demolishing the Kuan Hwa Mun, the central gate of the Kyungbok palace in Seoul – they were flawed because his appeal was aesthetically-based on a history of melancholy and nostalgia (we might say imbued with Western ideas of architectural heritage") – Kenjiro Okazaki (at the same *Anywise* conference) speculated that Yanagis interpretation came from his misunderstanding of the Korean concept of *han*, which generally means a deep sorrow and resentment at losing someone or something but, according to the famous Korean musician Chee Song Ja, also has the deeper meaning of the energy that comes from overcoming this pain. It is thus a sense of space rather than a sense of time. It is a sort of black hole or blankness – a space that all of history fills. It gives a positive motivation – it opens a way, as Benjamin would say, to let the wind through[8] – a suggestion I'll come back to shortly.

Tao Ho's projects and the debate they provoked also remind us that the value assigned to heritage can never be separated from present-day ideological fashions, political and economic imperatives. Heritage historians often claim that they work to prevent the disappearance of culturally significant objects, but in a way *they contribute to the very loss they seek to prevent*. They do not arrest change; rather they accelerate a re-evaluation that fixes the object in the past, and therefore secures its new status as cultural capital. To find the new value to be derived from the object it needs to be redefined as belonging to a history that has been lost. And these are the contradictions of an ideology, not a true reflection of that process of remembering – which, as Chee Song Ja attests, can embrace loss as a form of energy.

7   Ole Bouman, 'Letters to Anywise' in *Anywise*, p.246.
8   Kenjiro Okazaki, 'Responsibility' in *Anywise*, p.61.

9 Michael Thompson, *Rubbish Theory*   10 C. Northcote Parkinson, 'Suffolk House', Unpublished paper, n.d., Archives, Penang Library.

A few years ago sociologist Michael Thompson proposed an interesting model to explain this process. Besides objects in the durable category, [which] increase in value over time and have (ideally) infinite life-spans, and transient objects, which decrease in value over time and have finite life-spans, he identified a third covert category, which he called *rubbish*, occupying a region of flexibility. Rubbish, in his theory, was the category of change, providing the path for the seemingly impossible transfer of an object from transience to durability because, as he pointed out (and the cycles of fashion and taste illustrate) the transient does not usually disappear – it just continues to exist in a timeless and valueless limbo where at some later date (if it has not by that time turned or been made into dust) it has the chance of being discovered.[9]

That image of demolition is suggestive: as Thompson points out (and again as schemes of inner urban modernisation involving the wholescale clearance of traditional housing – now renamed as slums or rubbish – illustrate) houses may be one of the most durable forms of capital but they too can become obsolescent and, if not demolished first, enter the zone of zero-value and historical limbo which ruins share with rubbish. To enter the category of rubbish is clearly a perilous loss of prestige. But it also bestows certain privileges. For example it grants the object *invisibility*. The once famous house or church or mosque, now neglected, unroofed and overgrown with tropical vegetation, no longer *signifies*; it has passed out of the social imaginary and been forgotten. This makes it vulnerable: the ambitions of the developer may rapidly reduce it to dust.

On the other hand, having forfeited its category membership, floating in limbo, it is no longer bound to conform to socio-cultural expectations and die: it can hang on, it can even come back from the dead. This reappearance may be sudden – Thompson borrows the description of physical systems provided by chaos theory to show that in fact the social rebirth of an object, its rapidly upward re-evaluation, is never gradual but is the result of a rapid often traumatic overthrow of former value distinctions and associated behaviours. As regards built heritage, this phenomenon of instant re-evaluation is usually associated with a change of government or minister, as a result of which a reversal of policy occurs that could not have been predicted.

So much, then, for a definition of heritage as that which can be passed down unchanged from generation to generation; in reality the cultural heritage lobby only steps in where an object, usually a building, has *ceased* to be passed down and risks turning into rubbish. Furthermore, in preserving and restoring a structure deemed to be historically significant, the heritage historians do what architects do: they invoke an ideal form, a utopian image of what it might once have been like – take the case of the once-splendid, but now ruined Suffolk House, an early colonial mansion built on the outskirts of Georgetown, Penang around 1817. When its restoration was first proposed in the 1950s, it was suggested that the result would be to recreate an image of a vanished way of life: "It would make a new place of resort, recapturing the atmosphere of the old days when John Company ruled the island, when gentlemen drove in their curricles, when disputes might still be settled with pistols at fourteen paces and when Georgetown was quite as Georgian as its name would seem to imply."[10]

A more sophisticated proposal put forward a few years ago would incorporate Suffolk House into a linear park, linking it to other sites of cultural heritage significance,[11] but the essential concept of heritage *as historical theatre* remains unchanged. Restored as a heritage museum and heritage research centre, Suffolk House's post-1817 history would be lost. The process of gradual ruination, the co-existence on the abandoned site of other histories: all this would have to be forgotten so that "our" – that is to say, the ideologically approved – heritage could be remembered. To make Suffolk House appear in all its architectural glory, its history would have to be erased. This is what I call the *tabula rasa* mentality of architects: pretending to return to origins, they wipe out every evidence of historical process.

These contradictions arise wherever cultural heritage is identified with architecture. Take another scenario: members of a Chinese guild want to restore the guildhouse's leaking roof; to raise money they sell precious objects they possess. At this point, however, their attention is drawn to the heritage value of their movables, their furniture, instruments, costumes, carved relics. They are further reminded that the physical fabric of their building is as it were irreplaceable, and where the physical fabric is degraded should be restored as faithfully as possible – this, of course, will be expensive but they (the heritage lobby) will assist in fund-raising.

The result? A pragmatic repair job is transformed into a project to turn the guild's headquarters into a kind of living museum. Of course there was incomprehension among the guild members at first. It had to be explained that decayed fabric could not be torn down, thrown out and replaced with newly manufactured parts; and, as the heritage workers didnt speak Cantonese, much of this persuasion took place in a kind of sign-language ...but progress is being made.

Leaving aside the fundamental point – if the guild members (for whatever reason) have neither the vision nor the will to restore their headquarters, what purpose is served in coercing them into being their own custodians? – what happens in this process to the tradition, essential one might have thought to the maintenence of skills, of replace-ment? The craft guild's lack of nostalgia for old things, an interest purely in their utility, goes hand in hand with a confidence that they can be replaced. If they cannot be replaced, then the skills that managed change so skillfully and artfully also disappear. And this is exactly what happens when the heritage historian steps in. The craftsman becomes another figure in the heritage tableau, frozen like his building in the no-time of heritage. As for the "life" of the place, it has to be tidied up: no more illegal gambling as the tables are needed for a historical display – of playing cards perhaps!

This scenario not only shows the paternalism informing much heritage theory and practice: it also illustrates how heritage policies, by *theatricalising* the resident, turning him into a tourist entertainer, recapitulate the strategies of Western colonialism. In an action plan called Investing in the Past for the Future, conservation architects have recently proposed part of downtown Georgetown as the site for a craft market for traders affected by the repeal of the Rent Control Act: Traditional trades can be perpetuated at the subsidised market while the old premises could be used for other viable businesses (like *cafés*)."[12] But this is exactly how the East India Company operated! First, a people is displaced in order to create a new pool of unemployed labour; second, the same people, politically disenfranchised because spatially disempowered, now work for their masters. They will make furniture and knick-knacks to furnish the houses of the middle-classes – in all probability the very same houses that they themselves formerly occupied.

Suffolk House, Georgetown, Penang, July 1998.

13 Kenjiro Okazaki, 'Responsibility', p.60.

It seems to me that the future of cultural heritage depends on developing a different conception of the past. As long as it is conceived in terms of significant buildings, it continues to embody a rather European prejudice. Architecture is made the sole repository of social memory, and in the process all those other constituents of a localised historical identity which (as Solà-Morales points out) architectural analysis fails to address, are ignored. These other constituents are not monumental, and their life histories do not unfold along Thompson's axis. Rather than being artificially embalmed and fixed in the nowhere heritage time of the theatrical tableau, their vitality depends on repeated performance and, most fundamentally, on learning to embrace Chee Song Ja's insight, that loss is to be studied, looked after and embraced.

This is the point Okazaki makes when, with the German-Jewish critic of Modernism, Walter Benjamin, in mind, he argues that the place of urban design should be conceived *like a stage*: "The stage may be placed so that the events of the future are projected on the past or the events of the past are projected on the future; on the stage events are repeated and replayed."[13] Of course it all depends what is meant by a stage: a heritage museum stages the past, but it hardly fulfils Benjamin's desire "to open the way in every direction and let the wind go through." On the other hand a street, a shrine, a group of houses, a chain of squares held together by a festival or a procession is a stage in a different sense. Religious ceremonies, commemorative celebrations – indeed whatever social acts serve to ritualise the spaces of everyday life – may be said to enact a cultural heritage in a way *that is not self-consciously theatrical but sub-consciously performative.*

The performance of our everyday spaces is the means by which communities tie themselves together, instilling a sense of familiarity in their surroundings. Thinking of the importance which audition has in creating a sense of continuity in change, the "noise" of a market, a shop, a small factory or a temple precinct does not interfere with communication; on the contrary, it is consciously maintained as a way of "tuning" the environment. But essential to the sense of wellbeing that a performative space creates is its capapcity to reform itself continually: unlike the theatre, the spaces of everyday life remain fascinating because of *their margins of unpredictability.* They are not the passive containers of "tradition", but the places where the past is consciously being transformed into the future. They are, in short, sites where "loss" is embraced, and where what is slipping into the past is constantly caught up, transformed and remade.

In a sense the performances of everyday life, which are the means by which those dimensions of cultural heritage which architectural analysis cannot imagine remain constituents of the city's life, are like Thompson's "rubbish"; they are places where identities and meanings grow flexible, open to rearrangement and renegotiation. This is obviously the case where worshippers at religious festivals temporarily fall under the spell of the deity and seem to *put on* (etymologically, perform) new selves; but it is also a normal feature of that idle chatter that makes up the friendly noise of the bazaar – where the ordinary is constantly being transformed into the unique, the unrepeatable.

Top: Secret Ceremony, Suffolk House, 16 July 1998, members of Bharatam Dance Company, Melbourne and the Gendang Terinai Dance and Orchestra of Perlis (Video clip: Ettore Siracusa).
Above: Jadi Jadian, a studio performance by the Bharatam Dance Company based on secret ceremony at Suffolk House, The Malthouse, Melbourne, 3 October 1998.

That most heritage historians and conservationists would not even recognise the performative structures of everyday life as constituting a key mode of spatial inscription and place-making merely underlines how inadequate architecturally framed conceptions of cultural heritage are to describe the constituent parts of the life of the metropolis – or, for that matter, the life of the real, as opposed to ideal, village. But it may also illustrate how out of touch Western heritage theory and practice is with that South-East Asian "architecture without architects," a constellation of vernacular building traditions which, in sharp contrast with the self-contained, environmentally insulated European building, have always had as a primary object of their design to let the wind through.

Compare the regimented, environmentally alienated modern housing estate or condominium complex with the design of the traditional Malaysian *kampong*. As Lim Jee Yuan explains, the *kampong* is remarkable for its lack of clear boundaries. Houses are joined by free-flowing paths winding round the houses. House compounds flow into each other. Few obstructive physical barriers are used to demarcate territories. Instead, very subtle and unobtrusive markings are used. Fallen coconut tree trunks and a cleanly swept compound could already define a house compound. In the *kampong* the definition of public and private areas is unclear and overlaps.[14] The same author writes, "The wooden traditional Malay house raised on stilts exhibits a quality of openness which is unseen in most modern houses," even adding, "The quality of openness reflects the *importance given to ventilation* in the design of the Malay house."[15]

Similar observations apply throughout the region, to a Bidayuh longhouse, to the *Lingat* of the Tanimbar islands, or even to the rural villages of Tamil Nadu.[16] In these cultures architecture is understood performatively; building can be an end in itself, a socio-spatial ritual where every part of the process, dismantling an earlier structure, rededication of the site and re-assemblage are equally emphasised. Thus the prestige that attaches to a Toraja origin house depends on the number of times it has been rebuilt; similarly in northern Thailand it is *traditional* to transform the house as often as possible.[17] These performative conceptions or architecture are remote from the fixed in the eternal present heritage visions of Tao Ho or his critics, and they underline the point that in the South-East Asian context the preservation of those memory sites where the wind blows through does not mean a divorce from architecture; rather, it means freeing heritage discourse from an irrelevant, and destructive, conception of architectural form, and restoring to it a vocabulary, and analytical tools, derived from the performative reality of local vernacular building traditions.

It might be asked how a consciously planned intervention to consolidate these habits of cultural regeneration can avoid leading to Kurokawa's banally consumerist vision of different regions competing with one another for the tourist dollar. But the vital point to remember is that, in the vernacular traditions referred to here, a symbiosis between restoration and redevelopment already existed. The vitality of traditional societies in South-East Asia always depended on a capacity to mobilise built structures, to make them circulate in a cultural space performing a host of spatial, social, economic and political functions. Migration to the cities is nothing new. What is new is the denial of this mobility, this traditional capacity for communal self-renewal and performative retuning in the name of Western-style modernisation and its heritage museum view of the past.

14 Lim Jee Yuan, *The Malay House*, Institut Masyarakat, Penang, 1987, p.93.
15 Lim Jee Yuan, *The Malay House*, p.73, emphasis in original.
16 See, Roxana Waterford, *The Living House, an anthropology of architecture in South-East Asia*, Oxford University Press, Singapore, 1990, p. 59 and p.161 and Margaret Trawick, *Notes on Love in a Tamil Family*, University of California Press, Berkeley, 1995, p.87.
17 Roxana Waterford, *The Living House, an anthropology of architecture in South-East Asia*, p.232 and whole chapter 'Migrations'.

However much one tries to explain architecture in words, I do not think this is possible as it is only the final built object that can be judged, understood and liked or disliked.

Geoffrey Bawa has always been reticent about talking about his architecture and prefers instead to build and also to encourage people to experience the built work. However in a few rare interviews and writings he brings forth some insight into the thoughts and processes that seem to define his work.

Bawa has always seen the practice of architecture as an immensely personal thing in which one explores and puts together the various experiences and incidents in one's own life in response to given circumstances of client needs, site and available resources.

Obviously the architecture that one does comes out of two things – the need of the person and the types of materials available for use. Ultimately the rest comes out of yourself. You build what you think is an answer and which gives you pleasure. I think we all build for ourselves. At least you know what you want to do. It's not a theory or an intellectual answer.

His approach to architecture has always been one of direct experience and sensuousness. The prime concern is always for the life in the sequences of spaces that are created. His architecture does not engage the mind to be clever, but provides a background to an expected and anticipated life.

Essentially Bawa's architecture engages what already exists in either the natural landscape of a site or a functional necessity of accommodating necessary social events in a building, with an aesthetic intent which may be enjoyed by the user. He has never theorised about his work, instead left the theorising to others, although he admits that there is a theoretical content to the work.

That's for others to do. You can find strong theoretical ideas in the work. If someone else can just as easily see the point of the whole project, that is the theory.

Geoffrey Bawa ____

Bawa on Bawa

Lunuganga, the pot placed under a tree used to bring into focus an entire hill in the distance.

Dr. A.S.H. de Silva house in Galle. The house hugs the terrain and become one with it.

Such an understanding of theory rises out of Geoffrey Bawa's long and circuitous journey to becoming an architect at the relatively late age of 37. Before that he had read English and law at the University of Cambridge by the time he was 22. The years between, Bawa participated intimately in the carefree existence of the inter-war years in Europe and Sri Lanka. In those years he indulged and discovered the pleasures of life in which architecture – particularly gardens – was an integral part. First a slow grand tour through the Philippines and the United States, and then a long stay in Europe before he returned to Sri Lanka to look for the ideal piece of land to make his own paradise. In 1948 he bought a piece of land which he named LUNUGANGA (salt river), after the spectacular backwater that surrounds it, and settled down to make of it a garden that embodied the good life he had seen and experienced.

...Create something ...allude to that world, not recreate that world – because it was a different world, and you couldn't do it – be allied to it, ...It was not tied to any social structure except people enjoying themselves within their capability... Which was not alien to the life I led before going to England, (such as) at Kimbulapitiya (his grandfather's plantation in Negambo north of Colombo) and other places. It was marvelous sitting in this long veranda after lunch having endless conversations.

Here more than anything else shows his inimitable personal approach to moulding his immediate surroundings to give pleasure to its user. The essence of the garden predates his architectural training and nurtured his attitude to architecture without an overt theoretical justification for anything that was done. The process was one of serendipitous involvement with the landscape. A discovered view, a possible lowering of a hill to reveal another, and a building of another stair or another terrace, another sign of the hand of man.

I like human intervention, ... like in a landscape when people contrive to mould it to their moods.

It was enough that what was built or moulded managed to engage the user's mind in a pleasurable way. The natural environment is seen as almost as if it were clay in a sculptor's hand. This is moulded within its physical limits to produce a series of pleasing vistas, views and spaces. With simple geometric intervention, sometimes a mere line, Bawa 'civilises' the wildest stretch of jungle, and the careful placing of an artefact, in this case a pot placed in the middle distance under a tree, entire mountainsides are brought into focus. By carving out forests, lowering hills and draining marshes a carefully modulated configuration of space that allows for a variety of experiences, moods and even social possibility has been unveiled from what was the wildness of a tropical jungle and rubber plantation. The lessons learnt from these early experiments, which were a direct engagement with building and site to accommodate life, he maintained throughout his working life.

One of his earliest projects, the A.S.H. de Silva house (1963) in Galle uses the sloping site to great advantage. In the Kandalama hotel (1994) project in central Sri Lanka he has made a strict austere building stand out against the dramatic landscape. The vertical lines of the support structure and the horizontal planes of the floors, completely devoid of decoration, accentuate the landscape by letting it dominate and take over but with a strong sense of the hand of man still visible in the landscape. In the House on the Red Cliffs in Mirrissa (1997) he colonises a landscape by inserting into it a grid of columns and a sheltering roof that stands as a mere line in it. Space is seen as a continuum. All spaces adjacent and distant, whether used or unused are involved in the design. Sheltered and unsheltered space blends seamlessly and the room stretches out into the Antarctic.

Not so much rooms in rooms, but rooms in their context and seeing things beyond a particular room or space. Even as we are sitting here you can imagine how the place will change. One's feelings in a room constantly alter as one moves around it – particularly in the perception of outside and adjacent spaces. What I mean is that when you design anything – say that end wall there – you have to consider seeing through it, past it, around it from all different points of view. The landscape is a moving picture that one is inside of. It is a continuum in which all sides appear simultaneously.

Movement is very important. As you move through a building you are conscious of everything around you – although you may naturally see it in detail... the rooms are merely about orchestrating one's movement, determining how people move through space, because that really is what one does. Arrival being drawn in, discovering, being released to the view. The inter-linked spaces are backdrops to life. It is not a singular devotion to a to a beautiful view. There is a more intrinsic energy that goes on within the spaces whether sheltered or not.

What is there needs to be taken into consideration. Whether it annoys you or pleases you doesn't matter, you have to take it into consideration.

This attitude has meant that Bawa has always been deeply sceptical about form making for its own sake. Shown a design of an airport that had a strong form that suggested a bird and therefore flight and asked if he could do it

I don't know... I can never imagine it as a symbol. I can imagine it as a plan or a feeling of going through to an aeroplane. The final form comes from doing it, actually walking through... I have always been against making a shape and then having to be restricted by it.

In my approach to architecture I think my first concern is the arrangement of space. How this relates to the site and the needs of the moment within whatever constraints there are.

Even in his design for the Houses of Parliament at Sri Jayawardenapura (1982), the building which is in essence a monument and thus seemed to provide the agenda for a strong form, Bawa imagined various sequences of movement through the complex, particularly that of the central promenade that takes the speakers' procession from outer veranda to inner vestibule through to the end of the central chamber. Along with the other patterns of movement the building that results is a complex asymmetric form that breaks down the bulk of this vast complex, and is reminiscent of its historic predecessors in the royal and monastic buildings of Sri Lanka.

A major factor in defining his approach to design and the final design of a particular project is the site.

Obviously if you enjoy building you can't do it from an office. You have to go to the site because the site is altogether important. Whether it is a big building or a small building you must be involved with the site.

The site gives the most powerful push to a design along with the brief. Without seeing the site I cannot work. It is essential to be there. After two hours on the site, I have a mental picture of what will be there and how the site will change and that picture does not change.

After the initial picture has been established the process of building starts by trying to make others working with him to see the picture too.

...Getting the picture out and explaining to everyone is difficult. It is for this reason that the drawings we make, trees and all the landscape elements are included. They are about the total picture.

From the outset all drawings contain the salient physical features of the site including important trees and boulders and directions of views. The process of design and building is seen as an attempt to get as close as possible to the original picture that has developed in the mind, but with due consideration to how the site itself changes with the new impositions.

Cast concrete bass relief on the outer surface of the St. Thomas Preparatory School.

Concrete *Bries Soliel* use in the Bishops College classrooms.

The farm school in Hanwella, done for the Good Shepherd congregation with materials found in the area and assembled together with a definite aesthetic intent using local skills.

In each project one finds that one's thinking is unconfined. With the particular needs of the building at the back of one's mind one sees the solution as a totality – the site being all important – and one sees whatever vision is granted to one as a building set in its surroundings – the building seen from outside, the movement in the building, the whole picture one tries to see whatever anyone using the building would also see and feel. In short, the totality of appearance and movement in and out of the buildings.

This non-formal approach to design is extended to the execution on site as well. For Bawa, ultimate bliss is to see and participate in the building process directly on site. In an early project – Polontalawa (1964) – Bawa and Ulrik Plesner, partner and friend

...discovered a spot full of boulders and we both said how excellent and splendid it would be to build a house here. So we pulled some strings and sticks, brought some chairs and sandwiches, and built it with a contractor who followed every gesture of our hands.

He considers this close interaction with the craftsmen and technical personnel directly involved in making the buildings of the utmost importance.

...Sometimes quite often, they do much better than you expect them to. This trust is reflected in the buildings. The trust is also limited to ones intentions, which you must hold up to these craftsmen.

...There is also interaction with people and craftsmen – telling them what to do especially with the details. We do much more of this on the site than with drawings. The contribution of the makers, particularly the older carpenters and masons who are passionate about what they do is equal to or more in some cases than ours. It is always quite obvious they understand when we are talking about a detail on the site.

In other words the design is limited or extended by the knowledge and the resources of the craftsmen and technology available.

If what you want to build can't be built by you yourself, then you go to a master of that particular trade and say: "How do you do this?" Then they will tell you and then you have to work within those limitations.

...For instance, around the Madurai Club in India, you will see all over the place, marvelous instances of temples and little huts, all built of stone. All of which sets something ticking in your brain, thinking how they were all done and how I can do it. Then you talk to the stone cutters and the providers of stone on how you can best achieve your object. When you get that knowledge, then you design within it.

At the Madurai Club there was a lintel over a window that I wanted to be of stone. It was rather a wide slab, 12 ft x 2 ft. The master mason said that was easy and suggested to me to use bigger slabs on the floor because I had specified 4 ft x 2 ft and he could give me 8 ft x 3 ft or 1 ft x 10 ft. I thought that was very exciting and so changed the drawings and used the 8 ft x 3 ft slabs. I was so pleased with the lintel that I put another one on top of it just for fun!

The use of materials available in a locality has been of particular importance in his work throughout.

If you go to a tropical island, the architecture should be a way of building that comes from the island itself and from the people themselves.

A close look at all the buildings he has been involved in shows a great variety of attitudes to materials. The early buildings done through the firm of Edwards Ried and Begg of which he became a partner in 1958, show a textbook approach to the use of concrete. At St. Thomas Preparatory School (1964) and the Bishop's College (1965) simple concrete frame structures hold wide sunshades, corrugated roofs and brise-soleil. These early experiments made use of the ideas he was exposed to at the AA.

For St. Thomas there was a possibility of using reinforced concrete, which I was trained to do in a certain way and decorate in a certain way, using people who could, like Anil who was a good sculptor...

From these early experiences and experiments with frame structures, Bawa moved easily into the use of local materials available around him and the assembly of which was not conceptually dissimilar.

At the farm school he built in Hanwella for the Good Shepherd congregation in 1966, Bawa has achieved a humane modern complex of buildings using available local skills and materials – brick, plaster, coconut rafters and jungle posts. Mosaic work of broken plates donated by a nearby ceramic factory covers the walls. At the offices for the steel corporation (1967) he uses the potential for pre-cast concrete panels to great effect to build an airy breathing pavilion jutting out into a large pond. In the clubhouse built for Madurai Coats in Madurai, local stone splitting techniques and masonry skills are used to good effect along with recycled doors from old Chettinad houses.

I have built in India, Indonesia and Mauritius. They are all different in essence from what I do in Sri Lanka because all the materials used and the methods of construction are established in those countries. If you take the local materials and the general feel of the place into account, which I enjoyed doing, the resultant building automatically becomes regional. I do not make it regional and I do not take regionalism as a creed. I just build what I am asked to build.

What frightens me is that regionalism is thought to be a lessening of civilisation. It is not! Philip Johnson's house in Connecticut USA is as regional as a mud hut in wherever it lies. It is not a good thing to say, but it all comes from a lack of general education.

Each project is a very particular response to a culture it's in – particularly in respect to the materials. Understanding Bali is very different from South India. Stone is the material of South India and timber of Bali. Most decisions are obvious in that way. At least obvious to me. Design encompasses a cultural sensitivity. I respond to it through the site and the materials of the site. Any other response is bogus to me.

All this also implies the importance that is made to climate in the work. The material used and the forms that the craftsmen are capable of making have in them an intrinsic respect for the climate that they are in.

Materials and building techniques are seen as a consequence of availability and economy. There is no conscious effort to build in a vernacular or regional style but as a direct response to the climate and culture of the place. Through this attitude to architecture and building Bawa's work links the modern period to a continuum of history and building traditions of the regions and places he works in.

Bawa's skill at using the resources around him has also extended to people. From the brilliant mind of his long time partner, Dr. K. Poolagasundaram and a host of other architects, engineers and designers, master masons and metalworkers whose collaboration Bawa enjoys, he uses extensively and to advantage.

The essence of Bawa's work, the product of this process, is one in which form is articulated as a function of movement and experience of the context, either as grand landscape or tight urban space, enveloped in the materials and skills available to him. Architecture is seen as a line that defines and marks the presence of man in the landscape and then dissolves into the background to make way for life.

Above: Lunuganga, water garden.   Opposite: Lunuganga, the long view reminiscent of the Romantic tradition of English gardens.

The verandah at Lunuganga. The covered and uncovered spaces are seen as a continuum of the same space, again overcoming the dichotomy of inside and outside.

Above: In the Kandalama entrance, the outside and inside meld seamlessly together.   Opposite: The dramatic lines of the minimalist structure of the hotel stand out and accentuate the lines of the landscape.

The Madurai Club in India used local stone splitting and assembling techniques in the entire construction.

The house at Polontalawa done with a friend and partner Ulrik Plesner arose from a direct intervention in the lanscape with sticks, strings and gestures of the hand.

Working with a Master.

A personal note on the last ten years of Geoffrey Bawa's working life.
– Channa Daswatte

In 1989, Geoffrey Bawa turned 70. The work at the firm that he had been the partner of for 30 years, Edwards Ried and Begg, was at low ebb. Fame though, was already very much his lot, with the culminating event being an exhibition of his work at the Royal Institute of British Architects in 1985 and the publication of a monograph of his work. Bawa seemed to have done it all and there didn't seem to be anything left to say. Many thought that he would retire to his beloved Lunuganga, to contemplate the garden he had nurtured over the past 40 years. Nothing could have been further from the truth. For almost ten more years, until his working life was called to an abrupt halt due to two successive strokes that left him paralysed and speechless, Geoffrey Bawa embarked on a solo career, working from the annex to his house in Colombo with a group of young assistants for almost ten more years.

It started as a series of requests from people who had seen the published work in books and wanted Bawa to be involved in projects for the tourist industry that was seeing a boom in the Asian economy of the time. During the first two years of this period none of the projects except for

three houses were built under his supervision, but they left a superb collection of unbuilt drawings that record a rich collection of thoughts for leisure architecture.

Two projects from these stand out. In an extension to the Bali Hyatt, Bawa places a series of three types of villas in what would have been a bucolic setting of formalised rice paddy fields. Bawa is a master of contrasting the geometric with the natural. Casually placed villas line the geometric fields and a long swimming pool connected the reception area through the paddies to the large pool on the beach. The buildings themselves use the Balinese vernacular building materials and techniques to good contemporary effect.

For a project on the Indonesian island of Bintan, Bawa created a layout and master plan that incorporates umpteen types of villas, rooms and public areas that almost form a catalogue of ideas on leisure space design. Later the clients unable to build in the whole island changed the plans and Bawa dropped the idea.

An unusual project was a request by the Singapore Tourist Promotion Board

for a design for a green-house in the Singapore Botanic Gardens to accommodate a tropical cloud forest. Futuristic glass pyramids glittering above the treetops enclosed beautifully choreographed walks through a series of grottoes, paths and vistas. Unfortunately for Bawa here was a classic case of misunderstanding his *oeuvre*. Where Bawa was thought to be a 'vernacularist', the client expected a traditional colonial style greenhouse akin to the 19th century ones at Kew Gardens. The contemporary glass pyramids must have been a great surprise.

In 1989, Bawa was invited by the Currimjee family in Mauritius to design a house in Curepipe, a town in the hills in the centre of the island. For Bawa it was another opportunity to go to Mauritius where he had earlier built the Peter White house. Over the next six years and five site visits the house took shape under the watchful eye of the clients and another of their architect friends. In 1996, Bawa was invited to stay in the finished house as a houseguest.

The house is a series of solid flat roofed blocks that interlock to form a series of courts and partially enclosed garden spaces arranged on the

slope of a hill. Central to the whole composition is a corridor that passes through the main rooms disposed on the slope. The master suite and the private bedrooms are on the highest part of the site, the entry at mid level with main entertainment rooms placed further down the slope supported at the bottom by staff quarters and service areas. On entering the house from the stone paved driveway and *porte cochere*, the hall looks straight out at a stone court with formal planting. To the right side of this hall is a pool court across which is seen a fire reflected in the water, which is extremely effective in the cool sub tropical climate of Curepipe. To the left is a guest room and the entrance into the long corridor that leads to the private rooms. The corridor continues on the right with an evenly high ceiling to lead into the successively higher rooms that are the sitting room and the dinning room. The vista is completed with a view of the garden below and the sky above.

Although it took some eight years to build, the house in Curepipe was typical of the relationship that Bawa built up with many of his clients for whom he has designed houses. A deep attachment, affection and respect for each other

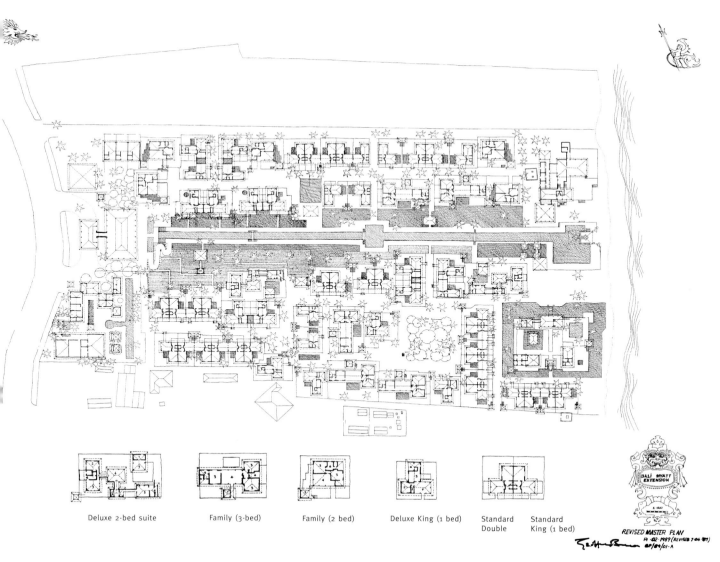

Deluxe 2-bed suite   Family (3-bed)   Family (2 bed)   Deluxe King (1 bed)   Standard Double   Standard King (1 bed)

REVISED MASTER PLAN
14·02·1989 (REVISED 7-04-'89)
08/09/01-A

Top: Bali Hyatt extension master plan   Bottom: Initial sketch for Currimjee house in Curepipe, Mauritius. The ground level is shown in blue with the upper floor indicated in red.

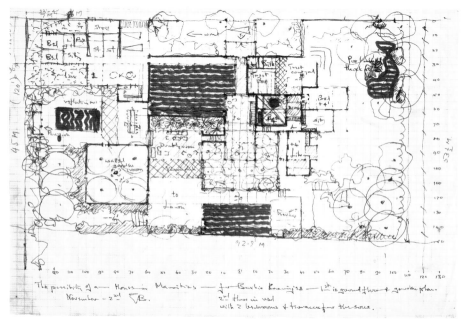

that allows the architecture to mature with them.

Bawa with Asker Moosajee, for whom he had built the Serendib a in 1970, had developed another such long-term relationship with the client. In 1990 Bawa visited an old hotel that Moosajee had bought. In spite of repeated warnings by friends, as to the dangers of taking such a thing on, Bawa took stick and string and threw himself wholeheartedly into the renovation of the public areas. Many a wall was built in the absence of the client with the assurance that he would never have it torn down! With his old mason, and the connivance of the then manager of the hotel, another long-standing friend, Bawa made a complete turn around to an otherwise dull and uninteresting building, opening up views into the hidden lagoon, creating a lagoon-side deck and adding the entrance pavilion makes this small

three-star hotel second to none that Bawa has designed.

Arising from this commission, The Sindbad Garden Hotel was designed in 1994. After many trial designs, none of which pleased him, Bawa came out with a unique possibility.

"The Sindbad occupies a relatively flat site and incorporates the original resort that sits at the end of the promontory controlled and claimed by the new complex. In order to establish a new arrival space at the scale of the site the new hotel encloses an existing grove of palms with a grand walled entry court. The corridors of the hotel are marshalled into a super-scaled spine or armature that provides the wall for the palm court and defines the principal spatial divisions within the public spaces of the hotel. The simple planning strategy is matched by great planes of the over sailing

pitched red tiled roofs that stand as the principal form in the landscape. As a counter point the suites are grouped into free standing villas that slip between the screens of pandanus and palms to further stitch the hotel into its idyllic setting."

*Michael Kinneger
Bawa-Recent Projects
1987-1995
Royal Australian Institute
of Architecture*

Initially this design seemed an improbable idea to sell to a client. A three-storied eight-foot wide corridor laid as a cross in the middle of the land seemed an outlandish proposal for a hotel. But the idea was sold and the construction commenced in 1994.

In 1990, the Aitken Spence group for whom he had already built two highly successful hotels, the Neptune (1974) and the Triton (1982) came to Bawa for advice on building a hotel in the interior of the island, in

the area now known as the Cultural Triangle. Here in a vast plain in the north central part of the island, in an area within a triangle joining the ancient, medieval and last capital of the Sinhalese kingdom, lie the cultural treasures of Sri Lanka. In the centre of this triangle is one of the gems of these sites the 5th century rock fortress and Gardens at Sigiriya.

The original site offered to the company was at the base of the huge rock of Sigiriya. Bawa was taken to a site allotted to the company which he later described as devoid of any charm as all the significant trees had been cut beforehand. He remembered from his various journeys across the country, a beautiful reservoir, the banks of which would make a good site. A drive cross-country to the tank bund of the 3rd century Kandalama tank, and a later helicopter ride helped identify the site of the Kandalama Hotel. The

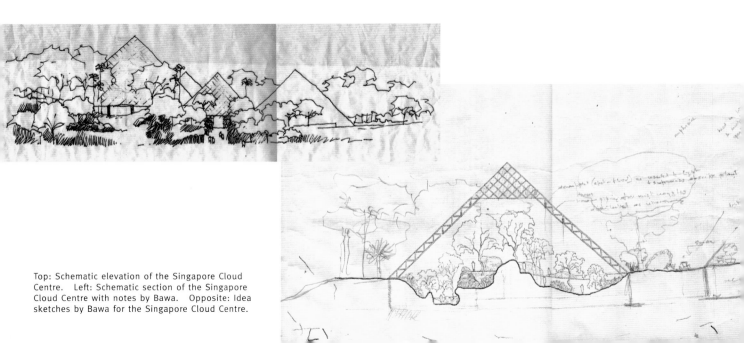

Top: Schematic elevation of the Singapore Cloud Centre.   Left: Schematic section of the Singapore Cloud Centre with notes by Bawa.   Opposite: Idea sketches by Bawa for the Singapore Cloud Centre.

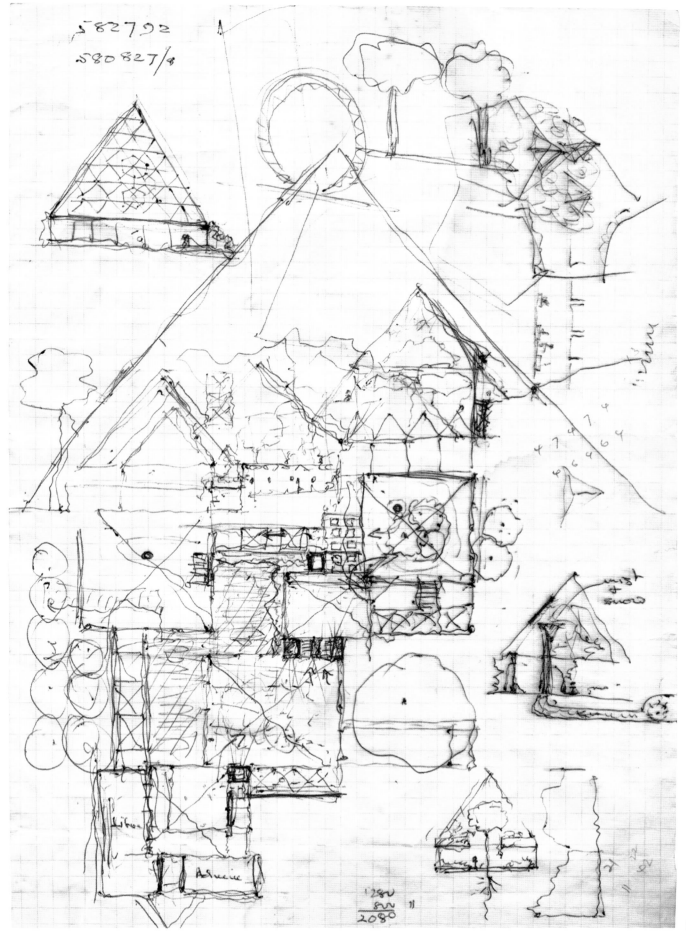

582792
580 827/9

57

early sketches show a conceptual idea not dissimilar to the nearby cave temples at Dambulla. But as it developed later, there arose a hotel that put all preconceptions of hotel design aside and in its place is a unique view of what a tropical jungle hotel should be. Bawa wanted here in the jungle, a belvedere and a 'hide' from which to view the magnificent landscape.

Conceptually the hotel is extremely simple. A huge man made ramp takes the visitor almost forty feet above the bed of the ancient tank to a rock ledge that is the reception. From here a tunnel cut in the living rock takes the visitor to another ledge from which to view the landscape with the rock of Sigiriya some ten kilometres away. A swimming pool in the middle distance appears to merge with the water of the tank bringing the landscape into the building.

"Throughout the building it is the experience of the landscape that dominates and its drama is amplified by the approach through the cave-like entry that leads to the mirror of the pool aligned to be visually one with the lake beyond. Bawa has responded to the majesty of the setting in a magnificent way."

Michael Kinneger
Bawa-Recent Projects
1987-1995
Royal Australian Institute
of Architecture

The need for the hotel in this significant location was vociferously contested by various quarters. The final plans were thus subject to close scrutiny by the government's central environmental authority. The permission to go ahead with construction was granted by the government only after an extended environmental impact assessment report was submitted and approved. The public concern with the environment was the beginning of a new awareness that has resulted in legislation being enforced even within other tourist areas and buildings. At the Kandalama Hotel no effort has been spared to make the impact of the hotel on the site minimal. The decision to make it a multi-storey building was taken so that the area that number of rooms may cover on the ground is restricted. The cascading roof terraces with indigenous planting reduce the thermal loads on the site and also provide nesting and foraging for birds. The raising of the hotel over the ground on piloti over most of its length allows the earth vegetation and water to pass freely without interference on the site.

"The Kandalama Hotel is a landmark in every sense except the literal. A building inconspicuous in the landscape, yet within totally dominated by that landscape, making everyone feel in contact with the great panorama of nature changing during the day and night and during the seasons. It is a tourist complex that offers every visitor the reality of a tropical dream yet treats its setting with deep consideration."

Micheal Brawne
Architectural Review
December 1995, Vol
CXCVIII No.1186

During the trying times of the Kandalama project, Bawa always retreated to his beloved Lunuganga to contemplate his lot and come back rejuvenated to face the next challenge. However this contemplation had nothing to do with just sitting around looking at the magnificent vistas and terraces he had created. He built another building. Weekend after weekend after a week of challenges, Bawa went to Lunuganga and created what was later called the Cinnamon Hill House on the cinnamon hill of his garden

Cinnamon Hill House started as an idea to populate the southern extremity of Lunuganga which up to then was occupied only by a lonely windmill and its accompanying water tank. About the same time Bawa also acquired two beautiful windows from an 18th C house that was being demolished for road widening. He needed something to hold them up!

The intention was to resurrect a pavilion on the foundations of an original workshop that stood there in the 1970s, and then attach to it two bedrooms that might then become a guesthouse for occasional artists and friends. The windows and an earlier client gift of a door would be made to stand in this new construction. From the beginnings of a pavilion the plan grew around the dense grove of trees that was the site. Strings were drawn and sticks placed on the floor to make the final plan so that all the trees on the site except one would be saved. The one that was cut became the base for a table that adorns the pavilion. The top is a discarded cement top with leaf impressions designed by Bawa for the Bentota beach hotel in 1969.

The house evolved through the process of surveying the site while designing, simultaneously. Whilst Bawa imposes or makes marks on the site with his buildings he is also sensitive to the changes that those marks make on the site and begins responding to the changed site. The sticks and strings are a mere guide to view the whole construction in three dimensions on the site and with the site, before it is built.

"Design for Bawa is an improvisation on the site rather than a premeditated execution that privileges abstract conceptualisation over an intuitive and natural connection with the 'place'."

Robert Powell
A+U: Architecture and
Urbanism, November 1996
No.314

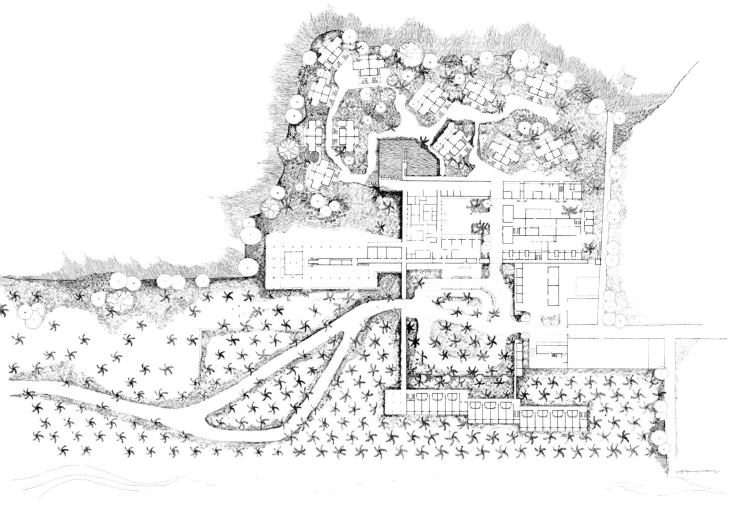

Top: Schematic plan for the Sindbad Garden Hotel.   Bottom: Plan of the House on the Cinnamon Hill, Lunuganga, Bentota.

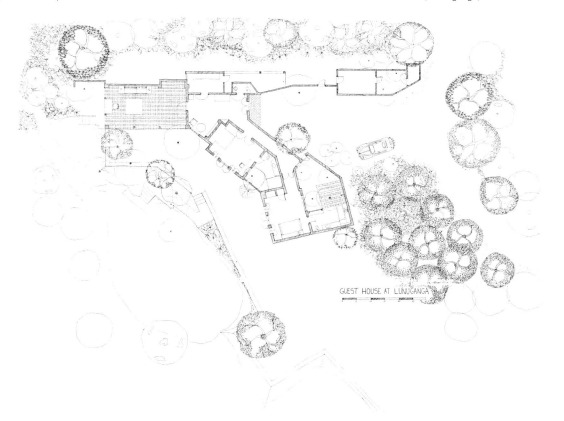

GUEST HOUSE AT LUNUGANGA

Another house built at the same time as the Cinnamon Hill House, but in a totally different setting is the Rohan Jayakody house in Colombo. Here on a site with an awkward configuration that had put off many buyers before the present owners, Bawa has made a house of immense tranquillity. A veritable oasis, in the middle of this otherwise very busy part of the inner city. The modest and restrained street elevation leads through a courtyard into a house of immense variety. From the main reception rooms onto the roof terraces with its emerald green swimming pool, the house has been seen as a 'microcosm of the city'.

"There is a choreography of space and light in complex interrelated patterns, overlapping and coalescing. A myriad moods and memories are condensed into a single house. Overall there is a feeling of immense calm and a sense of timelessness."

Robert Powell
The Urban Asian House –
Living in Tropical Cities,
Select Books 1998

The choreography of space and the immense calm of the Jayakody House are carried onto a windswept promontory, on the southwestern coast about a mile before the ancient port city of Galle. At the Lighthouse Hotel Bawa uses his mastery of promenade to negotiate a difficult site. The site placed tightly between sea and the main road to Galle from Colombo is also high above road level. Here a protracted entrance sequence is created to take the visitor up to the main level. The dark cool entrance veranda draws the visitor into the base of the hotel at road level. From there one is drawn into a cylindrical space, in which is a life-sized sculpture by Laki Senanayake of a battle between the Portuguese invaders and the islanders. This draws one up to the first level to be confronted by the glaring light of the veranda and the ceaseless crashing of waves on the rocks below.

The first block of bedrooms is placed on the edge of the sea. Along with a service block across from it on the road side, this defines a tranquil courtyard of tightly clipped grass that provides a counterpoint to the crashing of the waves. The second room block steps back to form a terrace by the sea that has a pool and the pool bar.

"The strategy is both to confront the relentless crashing of the waves and to provide contrasting areas of shelter and tranquillity.
No single space is self-contained or complete: each is part of and a consequence of a previous space and the anticipation of a subsequent one; each retains links wit its neighbours and with the outside so that the eye is continually invited to explore the

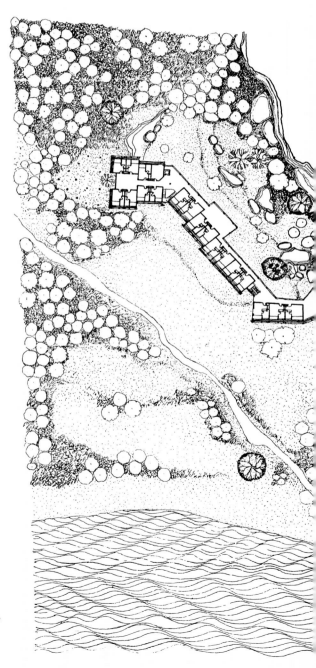

Plan of the Kandalama Hotel.

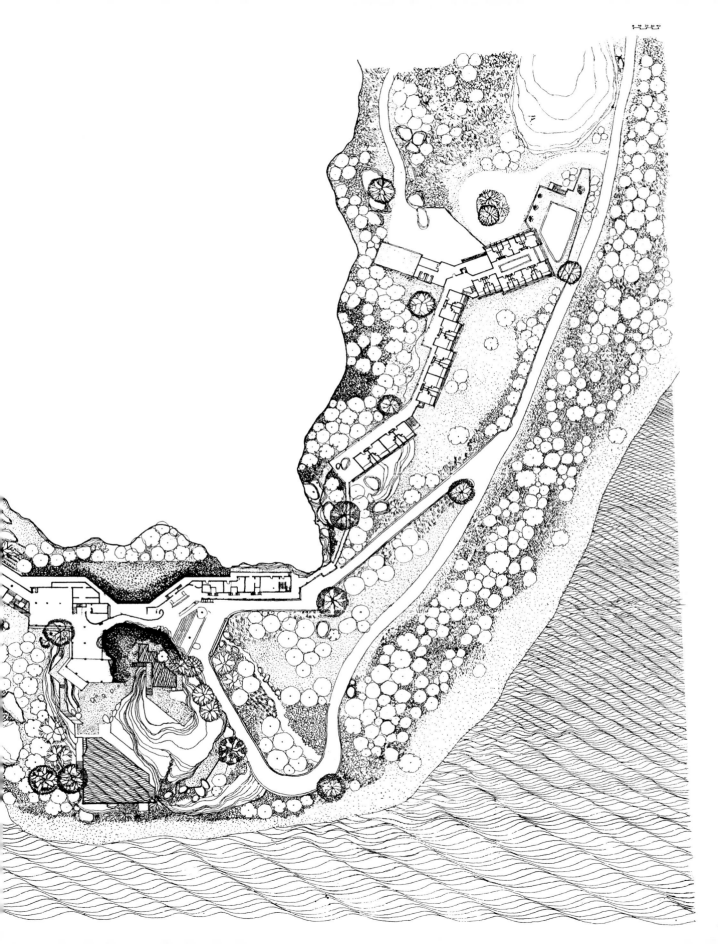

61

possibilities the building offers."

David Robson and Channa Daswatte "Serendip Serendipity – the architecture of Geoffrey Bawa" AA Files 35 Spring 1998

The client's requirement of a period hotel is met only in spirit. The austere and character of Dutch buildings is evoked in the spaces and through colour, along with the choice of heavy simply constructed furniture.

"The Lighthouse presents a picture of repose. There is a sense of ease in its presence, which makes design seem easy"

Ravin Gunaratne Lighthouse: Fired earth on aquamarine, Sri Lanka Architect Vol.101 No.20

For all his buildings, Bawa's initial impetus has always come from the site. The site generates the first impressions of the architecture that would be on it. One project in 1992 however deviated from this norm. A long fax from a lady in London was the impetus for working on a design for a house in the outskirts of Delhi. For Minal and Lalit Modi, Bawa designed a house even before he had seen the clients. For Bawa this is rare. His usual reactions to the site were made secondary by his fascination with the character of a person who might send a 10-page fax describing her dream house. He designed the house as an imagined event of his visiting her in it. When finally they met client and architect hit it off enormously and the house that was designed fitted perfectly to the requirements. Although much work was done in the ensuing year, this house was unfortunately not built, but from this has arisen an enduring friendship.

At about the same time, Bawa was shown the plans of a small caravanserai on the Hyderabad road about 25 kilometres from Bangalore. It was to be turned into a weekend home for the Poddar family. The site, the caravanserai that was lived in by an old Courtesan, consisted of a cyclopean wall circular in plan, a stepped well in the centre which was overlooked by a Hanuman temple and flat roofed colonnades, all of local granite. The wall was pieced by a highly elaborate gateway.

The brief called for a weekend home and a place to display an extensive collection of Contemporary Indian painting and sculpture. This was met by making the larger of the two stone pavilions on the site into the main living spaces for the family and the smaller into guestrooms. One of the features of the pavilion structures was a long ambulatory like section that connected the two more rectangular pieces one bigger than the other. Here Bawa uses his essence of promenade and vista to show to best effect the qualities of the existing ruin. Entry and circulation is made through the ambulatory, which heightens the sense of drama by only slowly revealing the spaces beyond. Having experienced the magnificent vista of the slightly curved colonnade, the visitor was to enter the main pavilions proper. Through a colonnaded hall the Hanuman temple and stepped well were then revealed. The 2.5-m grid of stone columns determines the positions and dimensions of the spaces and the placing of furniture which was mostly designed to be built into the structure.

Reminiscent of the old ruined caravanserai with its long ambulatory and endless colonnade is the Blue Water Hotel. This was the last hotel project Bawa was involved in and was completed soon after he fell ill in 1998. On a rectangular site with no special features, Bawa responds like at the Sindbad by creating his own context. Here an extensive use of water and endless colonnades that disappear in to the distance evokes a feeling of infinity and peace. The very restrained furnishing of the hotel heightens the feeling of space, lightness and quiet disturbed only by the sound of running water, the rustling of palms and the ceaseless roar of the Indian Ocean in the background.

In 1996, with his solo practice at a peak, three hotels on site with two other houses finishing, Bawa was called upon to design the state residence and secretariat for the head of government of Sri Lanka. For a site across from the houses of parliament, which he completed in 1982, Bawa designed a series of pavilions that will be reflected in the lake surrounding the parliament and complementing it. The scale here though is quite different and has a more intimate spatial arrangement as befits a residence. The secretariat was designed as an immense gatehouse to the high security complex and entered on a bridge across a canal.

The House on the Red Cliffs is perhaps Bawa's last completed work. Built on a spectacular site overlooking the Indian Ocean, the house appears merely as a line in the landscape. A huge metal roof on slender columns shelters the main living areas of the house on the summit of the site and the sleeping areas are tucked partly underground to shelter from the sweeping monsoon winds and open onto a shaded terrace on a more sheltered slope of the hill. A wind-scoop like entrance gives access to these spaces. Here architecture has been pared down to a minimum. There are no doors and windows to come before the view, no decoration to distract from it. The structure hies back to a primeval idea of shelter but articulated in contemporary materials and accommodating current sensibility. Here the formality of architecture recedes into

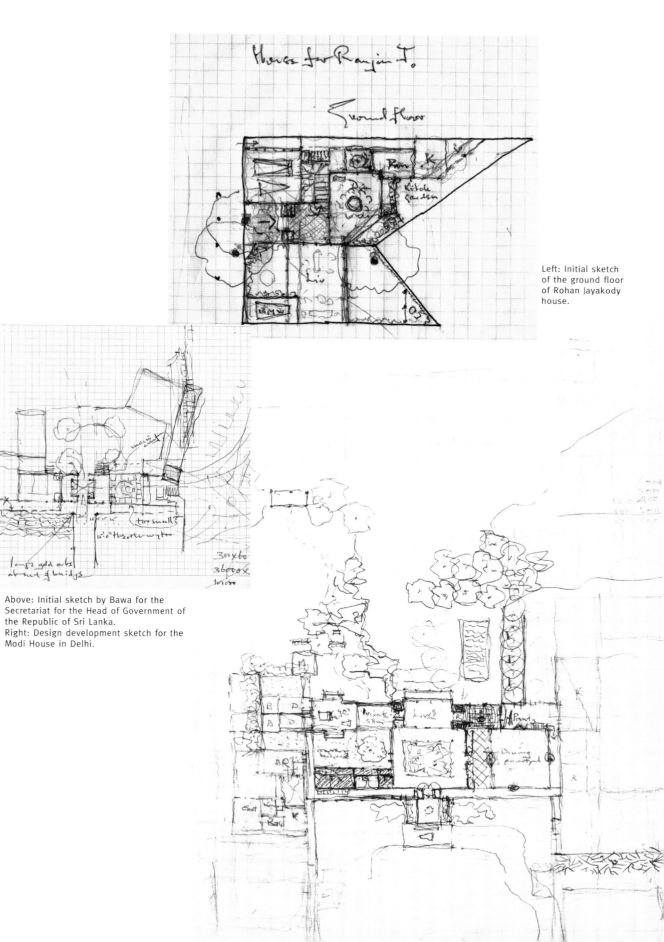

Left: Initial sketch
of the ground floor
of Rohan Jayakody
house.

Above: Initial sketch by Bawa for the
Secretariat for the Head of Government of
the Republic of Sri Lanka.
Right: Design development sketch for the
Modi House in Delhi.

the background, "one last footstep before formlessness."[1]

It has been said that a truly great work of art is never as rich as the person that created it. This most certainly applies to Geoffrey Bawa and his work. In person he is urbane, witty, and above all very humane. This made working with him an even more enriching experience. The office in his annexe never had more than six assistants at a time, and officially took on architectural work only up to the schematic phase of design. The truth however is that the office is always involved in every aspect of the finished product. Bawa advises on everything from the design of tables and chairs for his houses and hotels to the ashtrays and uniforms.

The intimate atmosphere in the a small space means that there is a lot of contact time between Bawa and the assistants who virtually work on top of each other. One moment there would be discussion of a particular aspect of the functioning of a dining room, and the next a large discarded blueprint would be spread on the ground to explain the finer points of the shape of a chair in full scale to a craftsman. Throughout his career Bawa worked with his trusted friends who provided their artistic skills to adorn his buildings and many of his early associates continued to work with him. All through this time a

cavalcade of humanity – artists, architects, craftsmen and engineers, suppliers and contractors – passed through the office not only providing the various services that were required of them, but enriching it with their personalities and experience. Bawa presided over all this from the round table over which he designed on his characteristic blue squared pad. However, like his buildings he never imposes on anybody. Even the youngest and most recent of the assistants has equally direct access to him, and any mistake was corrected with a characteristic "wouldn't it be better if we did it this way". Again, like his architecture, Bawa stepped back and allowed for the youthful enthusiasm and life of the office. However his is the final word, said gently but firmly to reign in the excesses of youth with his wisdom and experience. Again like his architecture, which celebrated above all else human engagement with it, working for Bawa is a constant celebration of the possibilities for life that could be made through the architecture the office produces.

1   From a poem "House on the red cliffs" by Michael Ondaatje.

Right: House on the Red Cliffs – concept sketch by Bawa.
Opposite: Plan of the conversion of the Chikkajhalla fort for the Poddar House.

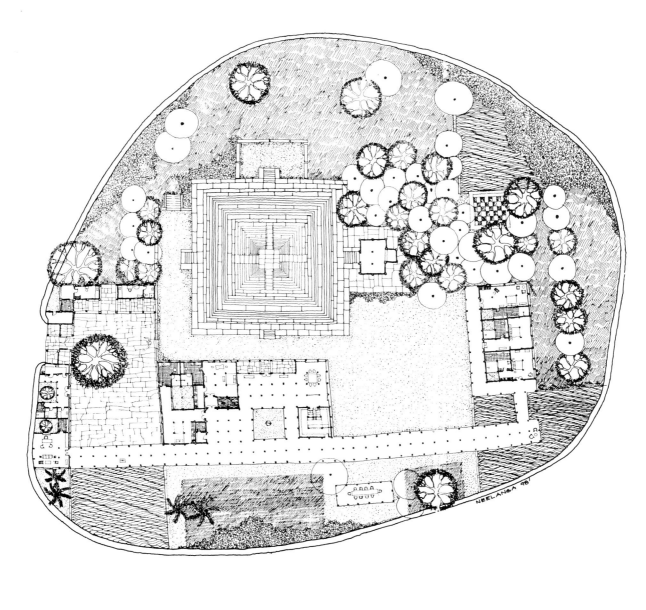

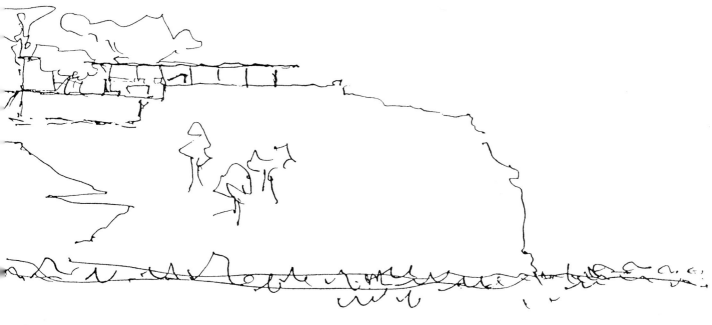

Nanjing, 1943. This was 1943 in Nanjing, before my father was put in prison. This was taken in the garden of our house. The year after, we were living in a mud hut. I'm wearing an aluminium cap, after being kicked by a horse. It was miracle that I survived. I was rushed to a hospital that my father has just built.

Teenage years in Hong Kong. (Hong Kong, 1955) This was 1955, the year before I went to the States, with my father, mother and my sister Diana. My mother had a degree in economics from Guangzhou but she never worked, except as a housewife. We didn't have any money but my brother, my sister and I all won scholarships to the States.

Presentation of Graduate Thesis Project, April 1964, Harvard. Standing, left to right: Walter Bogner, Tao Ho, Sigfried Giedion. Seated at left: Eduard Sekler, Jose Luis Sert. Siegfried Giedon was very important to me. I was his personal assistant to do illustrations for his last book, *The Beginning of Architecture*. He was toiling with the contradiction between constancy and change. In the human spirit there is a constant reaching out for artistic expression, forever refining our environment. Each period has its own expression. He described to me what he saw in an Egyptian tomb and I had to sketch it out. It would go on for days and days until I got what he was looking for. He was a very nice, very humble person but gave me hell if I gave him something which wasn't what he wanted. After work he would bring out a bottle of sherry and talk about philosophy.

Tao Ho

Working with Invisible Form

as told by Tao Ho to Ralph Thomas

Foreign Correspondents Club
In late '67 I was asked if I would like to do an interior design proposal for the Foreign Corre-spondents' Club. That was a big break. Going to Harvard, you don't learn how to do details. I learned the hard way. It was design and build. I did the whole set of working drawings myself. I used rope to make screens, beer cans to make downlights, beer bottles with lighting behind, for the bar counter. It was crazy stuff.

Hung Hom Exhibition, Hong Kong Govt pavilion (1971) In 1970 I was asked by the Government Information Service to do a competition for a Hong Kong Government pavilion at the Hung Hom trade fair. I designed a pavilion with open sides, sym-bolising open government. Display material was mounted on the inside of a series of drums re-presenting government departments, suspended at high level. I won the competition.
Hung Hom Exhibition, Olivetti pavilion
Visitors walked through an inclined space on a precast walkway, surrounded by a chequer-board of mirrors, inter-spersed with product display. It was very small but felt bigger than it was.

Patriotism & Culture

I feel more Chinese than the average person from Hong Kong. I don't blame some Hong Kong people for not accepting China as their country. For the average Hong Kong person it's very difficult, because of the lack of under-standing. My patriotism is because of my childhood in China, my classical education. Patriotism is respect for your own cultural heritage.

Cultural heritage and tradition have two aspects. One is the software, the invisible aspect. The other is the hardware, the visible, tangible aspect.

Software is the rooted tradition of a culture. Five hundred years before Confucius there was Zhou Kung. He set the moral framework for Chinese culture. Then there was Confucius and Lao Tzu. They shaped two contrasting strains of Chinese culture. The first is formal, the second informal. Both are part of my roots. These invisible roots of a culture operate in a similar way to what Carl Jung calls the collective unconscious.

When it comes to the visible part, the hardware of culture, the software manifests itself in different ways, in different places at different times. It's dynamic, in the sense that it evolves, although the basic spirit remains pretty constant.

Formality and Informality in China

The two software systems of Chinese culture produce two distinct categories of hardware.

In the formal and ritualistic approach defined by Confucius, everything is part of a modular system defined by a hierarchy. You end up with the Palace, the courtyard houses, the head of the family always in the same place in the house. This is one strong aspect of Chinese architecture: symmetry, formality, a hierarchy of spatial sequences.

Fortunately, the influence of Confucianism is counterbalanced by the informality of Taoism: hidden surprises, asymmetry, reflection of nature. That you can see in the Emperor's private quarters in the rear of the Palace in Beijing, which is totally informal. The archetype of this is the gardens of Suzhou. Each one has its own character. One is full of rocks, another full of plants, another of water.

Throughout Chinese history, architectural form has reflected this constant interaction of formality and informality.

Solid & Void

When it gets to modern architecture, working for Gropius inspired me to express the deep roots of Chinese

Bucky on Delos with Doxiadis (1974) In 1974, I was invited to attend a symposium on the Greek island of Delos by C.A. Doxiadis, the Greek visionary and city planner. I was the youngest there, amongst the heroic figures of the time. It was very simple and informal. We ate together in a Greek village. We formulated ideas for human settlement and made a declaration, in the manner of CIAM.
With Buckminster Fuller, (1975) On Delos I met Bucky Fuller, to whom I became very close. His visionary ideas became deeply rooted in my mind. You don't have those kinds of people anymore. They talked about the world, how to save the world, romantic as it sounds. That heroic sense has gone. Architecture today has become another business, which is sad.

Hong Kong International Elementary School (1975) Overall exterior: My first big job was the International Elementary School. While I was at Harvard, they were talking about open team teaching methods, without classrooms. Professors from the Education Department came to talk to us about this new philosophy of team teaching. Almost ten years later my client was very pleased that I understood team teaching.
Rainbow staircase: I wanted to enclose the staircase, to prevent children climbing over. I used vertical tubes, painted in a cycle of 36 colours. We also used super-graphics, trying to create a lively, playful environment for the kids. It was quite new at that time.

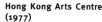

Hong Kong Arts Centre (1977)
Overall view: In '69, I collaborated with an enlightened government servant called Bill Bailey. We started the idea of the Hong Kong Arts Centre, which would be something like the Bauhaus in that it would incorporate all the arts in one building. Governor Maclehose came to Hong Kong in '72. He had a vision for Hong Kong. He was concerned about the quality of life here. We managed to get the Government to give us a piece of land. It was only 30 m x 30 m, with party walls on two sides and a corner chopped off. I told him it was too small. He said, "You're damned lucky to get a site!" We managed to fit in a gallery, theatre, music hall, practice rooms, restaurants and office space.
Atrium, view downwards: The staircase in the Atrium links all the public levels, up to the fifth floor. I made the carpet a major feature, defining a colour for each floor and mixing the proportion of colours between floors. Despite being hand-tufted, it cost the same as a standard, machine-made carpet.
Recital Hall: Here, I used strong colour. The Lyric Theatre was green. The Recital Hall was red, as a contrast. It's like being in the womb.
Sectional perspective: The building has two sides with no windows, which are party walls. They are treated as double walls, containing services and circulation. Within these is a triangle of usable space with only a couple of columns. Functions are stacked vertically. On the upper floors is a triangular void in the centre of the building above the fly tower.
View upwards (opposite): At the Arts Centre everything is exposed. Everything contributes to the design. I exposed the structure and in the middle of the atrium, an air conditioning duct hangs in the middle of the space.

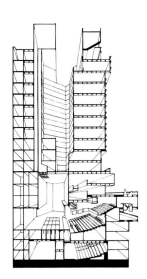

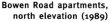

Bowen Road apartments, north elevation (1989)
In the early eighties, I was asked to design a residential development on Bowen Road. I was totally disgusted by the monotony of residential design in Hong Kong: twenty storey towers with forty units, exactly the same. There's no choice for people. I got inspiration from the illegal structures which people attach outside buildings.
Detail of elevation (1983)
The exterior form of the building aims to capture the variety of the internal arrangements.
Hong Kong Illegal Structures
Hong Kong illegal structures are a typical expression of self-organisation.

Vancouver Expo, Hong Kong Pavilion (1986) I did the Hong Kong Expo Pavilion in Vancouver in '86. That took advantage of my multi-disciplinary approach. The outside form of the pavilion was a yellow box, wrapped around with bamboo.

I employed two scaffolders from Hong Kong to stay in Vancouver for six months, taking down parts of the scaffolding and putting it back up, symbolising the constant reconstruction of Hong Kong. Inside, we had a huge back-projection screen (4 x 16 m)], depicting a day in Hong Kong, using 9,000 slides. I wrote the script, I commissioned Dominig Lam to write a piece of music to co-ordinate with the images, and Lo King Man directed the dancers. This was the first time that I mixed architecture, drama and music. I learned a great deal from that. As an artist I'm not limited to one medium.

Architects Container Office (1989) Entrance view: I'd always wanted to have an office on a boat. It wasn't really feasible. I went to site offices all the time. They were always in containers. When we bought a piece of land in Kowloon Tong, near the MTR, I just assembled 24 shipping containers. There were no foundations. The containers were not even fixed. The infill panels are not structural and can be opened up. On external walls, we put timber battens with glass fibre insulation, covered with plywood. I turned an existing garage into my conference room. **Interior view:** It's a typical Chinese court-yard scheme, on two levels, with a roof over the courtyard, which created a thermal stack effect. It was very ecologically efficient, creating a thermal stack effect in warm weather, drawing cool air through the building. It turned into a very lively office with the atrium as the village square. **Bamboo:** I planted bamboo in front of the east elevation. Glass laminated with glass fibre caught the shadows of the bamboo, like an animated Chinese painting. I left one pane clear, to let in reality.

tradition. Modern architecture is not just Western. It has Eastern roots as well.

Unfortunately a lot of Modern architecture has ignored environmental context and climatic conditions. Gropius wanted very much that those should be taken into consideration.

Recent Work in China

On Mount Qing Long, the local government wanted vacation houses to blend with the surroundings. My approach was contextual. I built them like farmhouses, planned in a way suitable for modern usage.

Why not revive classical Chinese architecture in sensitive historic areas? What's wrong with reading a Tang dynasty poem to seek inspiration for modern architecture?

It's sad but heritage is subject to supply and demand. If there's no demand, it will die out. If we speed up the process by cutting off supply, I think that's wrong. I would like to do my best to represent and propagate heritage in a dynamic manner. This means that when I renovate a heritage building I don't want to mummify the past, I want to revitalise it. The past is a living power.

Black's Link Housing (1987)
Overall view from below: Black's Link was built on a thirty-degree hillside. The normal Hong Kong response is to excavate a flat site, protected by a retaining wall. I conceived the idea of a series of tree houses, each supported by four extended caissons, linked by a pile cap platform. The slope beneath is landscaped.
Open space beneath housing. View up from the landscaped garden: Three of the houses are at lower level, reached by elevator. By adopting my proposal, the developer saved a lot of money and one year of construction time and government approval.

New Ink Painting, Impromptu in black ink on paper (1999) I'm currently exploring the expressive potential of Chinese ink with water, bleach and repellent materials. Like life, I am in control of part of it. The rest is self-organising. This principle is also common to my architecture and urban planning.
Top: Guilin, sketch, ink on paper (1990) I went to Guilin with my wife and daughter for a week and produced over fifty ink paintings.

Human history is like a chain from the past into the future. It's irresponsible to ignore history, to cut the chain.

Picking up the Paintbrush

A painter like Huang Bing-Hong (1864-1955) is a link in the chain. His work is a graphic representation of Chinese philosophy, particularly Taoism. He said, "A good painting is built upon method, yet without a method." It looks chaotic but it is ordered. It's free because all the method is second nature. There is order within chaos and chaos within order.

In October 1989 I was helping a friend to organise the first American exhibition of the work of Huang Bing-Hong at Williams College. I was invited there to give an opening talk. It was beautiful at that time of year. In the museum I bought a little sketchbook to sketch the woods. From that time I regained my creativity for painting. According to Huang Bing-Hong, you should let your hand be guided by your heart. After nearly thirty years, I started to paint again. That helped liberate my architecture too.

Form does not Follow Function

We make a big fuss about the style of a building. What a building looks like doesn't change its function. I can give a plan many stylistic forms. I try to choose a form which relates to the context. Wherever I work, I try to understand the culture and try not to cut off the past.

I was once asked by the Party Secretary of Shanghai what was the most difficult issue to address in the course of modernisation. I told him that it was the replacement of old buildings with inferior new ones. For a time they thought of demolishing the Bund. I helped convince them not to. It's part of your heritage, whether you like it or not. You can't blame your grandmother for being Eurasian.

Cultural Diversity

I don't agree with Mies. He had one architectural form to solve all the architectural problems of Planet Earth. I believe that more cannot be expressed with less. When you are dealing with diverse cultural patterns, I don't think that you can have one solution. Physically and emotionally we need more.

Religion & Architecture

Asian identity should not be an artificial thing. Asian identity is our attitude to the world. Those aspects of Asian identity shaped by Buddhism and Taoism seek union with the cosmos. The central

Xiamen Urban Planning, Model (1985)
In late '84 I was invited to do planning for Xiamen, one of the earliest free economic zones. I led an integrated team, together with colleagues from Great Earth. Our job was to develop strategies to cope with the impact of free trade across the whole of Xiamen Bay, taking account of local scale.

Mount Qianlong (1989)
On Mount Qing Long, the local government wanted vacation houses to blend with the surroundings. I built them like local houses. They didn't want this place visible from the West Lake, so it's hidden in the trees. I created running water in the middle, surrounded by the vacation houses, with a spa at one end.

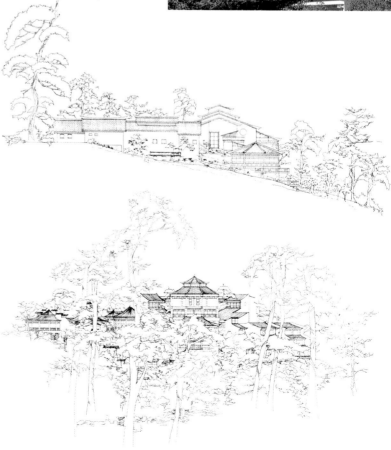

Suzhou Universal Centre (1994)

Model: In Suzhou, the Venice of the East, I was asked to build a commercial and entertainment complex right next to one and two storey traditional buildings in the middle of the old town. The city has gone through a continuous process of metamorphosis. For 2,500 years this has produced variations on a theme. Now there's a totally different piece of music. The city is undergoing a tremendous modernisation. The ancient spirit can disappear in no time, if decisive measures are not taken.

Sectional perspective: The building has a central void. In summer this is vented, allowing rising air to pull cool air through the building. In winter it is sealed, retaining a layer of hot air as a thermal buffer.

Old Suzhou: The scale of old Suzhou is one and two storeys, with interlocking elements, created by the response to practical needs. This spirit inspired my design.

theme of those philosophies is the acceptance of man as part of nature, to see the world in a holistic way, rather than as a composition of parts. The predominant Western way is to see the world as a synthesis of parts.

East Meets West

We share the same earth but we developed differently due to geographic separation. It's only in the 20th century that we've come together. Now is the time to harmonise the diversity in human culture. Forget about East and West. It's just like different dialects of the same language. In my work I try to put these two together. I use columns and beams. That's a universal law. I don't care whether they're Chinese or not.

I'm an ecumenical Christian. I accept the validity of other religions but I find the teaching of Christ more applicable to my life. I find Hinduism and Buddhism fascinating. The concept of time and space, of infinitely large and infinitely small, how that relates to the human being. They are about personal liberation. However, as an architect, I don't find them positive enough, not actively seeking change. I need to reach out to the world, not to escape from it.

The Interplay of Cultures

I'm a globalist. Globalisation is an inevitable part of human evolution. I see the world as one human culture, but I see the variety of it and I think that it should be protected. You don't have to unify everything. There's no need. We're in an age when America is on top. America can suffocate local Asian cultures. I'm not anti-American, but I'm concerned that this is having an ill effect on human heritage. We should take care what we hand down to our children.

I'm not a stylist. I'm not motivated by any stylistic form. Too many architects and artists are the victims of stylistic form. I'm against architecture as fashion. I hate deconstructivism, post Modernism. When I paint, I don't have any preconceived formulation.

Head vs Heart

In my recent painting I'm creating an imagery which is seemingly accidental but is actually guided by me. It's a difficult balance. It's the interaction of ink, of water and the natural repellence of materials. What I can control is where to put the materials, but I cannot predict their movement. I use bleach, which makes the ink disintegrate. I control the drying and movement of the ink with a hair-dryer.

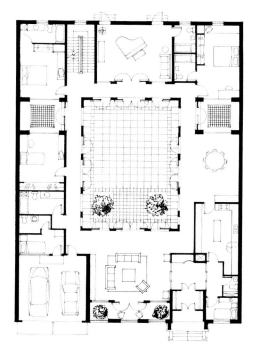

Courtyard houses, Beijing (1995) Exterior view: In Beijing, I developed some courtyard houses to harmonise with a neighbourhood originally occupied by the uncles of the Emperor. They look just like traditional Beijing houses. I see no reason not to use traditional forms with a modern plan. The courtyard house is adaptable to modern living. It would be wrong for me to use this form anywhere else.
Plan: Although the expression is inspired by tradition, the plan of my Beijing houses could belong to a wholly modern building.

King Tower, Shanghai, view across fields (1996)
In the Pudong district of Shanghai, there is no heritage to consider. Anything is permissible, so long as it is functionally viable, appropriate to the climatic conditions. At King Tower, my client asked me to create something heroic as the headquarters of the Jin Qiao Reprocessing Zone. He wanted it to be visible from afar, rising out of the flat ground. I didn't consider Chinese traditional style in a literal sense. I set out to give new definition to tall buildings.

Lobby interior: My client wanted a grand entrance. It's very spacious and full of light. I gave him a huge, glazed rainshield, extending up the front of the building, which also acts as a heat shield.

Head of tower (opposite): Hopefully, the building will look different from different angles. I tried to create many facets. Each facet will catch the light, changing throughout the day. In order to get more height, to satisfy the urge for a tall building, I continued the steel structure up to create a pyramid form. In a subconscious way the top of the building may have resemblance to a pagoda. To me, that's added value but it's not a conscious effort to make it Chinese.

You create a natural happening, a controlled phenomenon. You have to know when to stop. It's like urban planning, where you need to incorporate the dynamic self-organisation of life.

As an architect, you've got to be an artist as well. You have to understand scale, form, colour, texture. After the functional analysis, architecture is an art form. You can only be spontaneous after you have understood the functional requirements.

I don't know what my next building will look like. I first design a building framework of permanent elements, into which changeable elements can be slotted, like books on a shelf. The permanent elements are the structure, circulation, building services. The changeable things are the functional areas. I always think of end users. Then I try to create a spatial organisation that will elevate them above the norm. It is the job of the architect to elevate the quality of life.

Each situation gives me a different feeling. Each of my buildings carries a message. I call it the Invisible form. I think that today's architects place too much attention to the visible form; the geometry. I don't believe that visible form is the most important thing.

Hong Kong Today and Tomorrow

The Hong Kong Government has a way of creating policies to shape visual form. When they control too much, they stifle life. The liveliness of Hong Kong heritage; eating on the street, singing on the street, fortune tellers, they're all disappearing or being forced into a sterile environment. The Government should provide a framework for life to flourish. The law should protect life, not restrict or destroy it. I am a great believer in the dynamic, self-organising approach to life which I saw in China as a kid in the gutter.

Environmental Consciousness

Ecology is an Eastern tradition which should be better understood in Asia. Feng shui is very environmentally sensitive. It's a theory seeking balance between man and nature. We should not be opposed to nature.

What concerns me a lot is that it's very difficult to make buildings environmentally friendly here. They should be designed to relate to the climate in the region. Hong Kong is subject to conditions which are different from New York or Beijing or London. We're humid, hot and we have strong sun. These aren't taken into account because developers see no tangible gain in creating

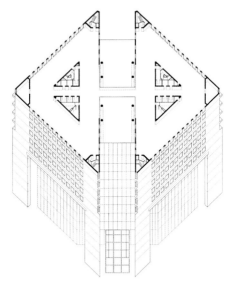

Construction Bank of China Headquarters, Beijing (1997)
Model: The original idea of the Construction Bank building was a black solid with a void through the middle. The void would be enclosed with low-E glass. At night it would light up, like a crystal. Beijing is formal, hierarchical. This is also the spirit of the bank. It had to be dignified, stable, reassuring. It's an honour to work on such a prestigious project.
Shang dynasty bronze: I drew inspiration from a Shang dynasty bronze ding. The Construction Bank has long spans, surface demarcation for windows.
Beijing gatehouse: I was also inspired by this Beijing gatehouse.

responsible buildings. More than ten years ago I made the Government a proposal. I said, Why not offer an incentive system to developers? If we can design energy efficient buildings by sun shading, then we should have some bonuses for the developer. I'm still fighting for that.

Putting Energy into the System

When 1997 came, it was suggested that I run for presidency of the Hong Kong Institute of Architects. When I was elected, I spent more than half my time working for the Institute. I'm always the Devil's advocate. What I'm against is conservatism. I'm not afraid to upset the Government. Two months after I became President, I opened my big mouth about the design proposals for our new Central Library. I was not criticising the design. I was criticising the system in which the design is produced.

Hong Kong is conservative. What has been done before, they keep on doing it. Design decisions are often made by the developer's junior staff, who have little scope for initiative. They don't believe that innovation is in their interests.

In Hong Kong, we need to shift the style of our practice, so that the quality of design is encouraged and rewarded. Hong Kong has a situation like

Apex Performance Venue, overall perspective (1998)
This design is the result of a feasibility study for a performance venue in Hong Kong. The Tourist Association wished to promote Hong Kong as the event capital of Asia. The job included identifying the most suitable site, analysing planning implications, undertaking statistical analysis of demand and economic feasibility and developing a design solution. It took a year to do the analysis. We found out that Hong Kong needs a well equipped, two thousand seat, proscenium arch theatre and a multi-purpose performing facility for 6,000 to 8,000 people. The normal way to do this in Hong Kong is just to fill these needs. I thought that we should also create a landmark. One of the unique features of the multi-purpose performance hall is a retractable glazed wall exploiting the backdrop of Victoria Harbour and the Peak.

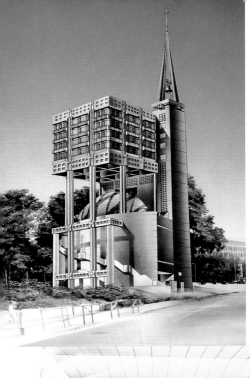

Wing Kwong Pentecostal Holiness Church, exterior view (1999): For Wing Kwong Church, the site is not so big and the elements are stacked. The main spatial element is a large auditorium for Sunday service. There's also a small chapel for more intimate gatherings. It's a very active church in a housing area. It's reaching out to the community. They need a lot of church offices. We put those on top. In the lease, the church had the money to build much higher but they only had the money to build what they need now. We've planned the building so that additional office floors for rent can be added later.

Auditorium, interior view: In the auditorium there will be a narrow slot in the shape of a cross which will throw light across the congregation in the morning. The altar wall will be glass blocks, in colours, getting lighter towards a cross in the centre, which will be clear, through which you can see the world.

Chapel, interior view: In the chapel there will be six strips of stained glass, running across the ceiling, representing the six days of creation. The seventh day is represented by the chapel itself. Humble materials are used expressively to communicate a sense of spirituality.

freemasonry. We should not make the HKIA a protectionist group. We should not make examinations a means to protect local graduates. We should be open to competition, particularly from mainland China.

Hong Kong has had twenty good years. The economy is built on the stock market and the property market. Those were at an unsustainable level. The unhealthy thing is that too many architectural firms have grown to keep up with demand. Some have hundreds of people. They have become bubble practices. It reminds me that in natural history, we went through 160 million years when dinosaurs ruled the world. The dinosaurs built up an unsustainable ecosystem. When climatic conditions changed, it collapsed overnight, about 65 million years ago. Our dinosaurs are the big developers. Developers want architects to have a big production office. The government also will only give work to large firms. They're looking for a smooth process, rather than an inspiring end product. Hong Kong architecture is trapped by the need for smooth processing.

I stick out in this society like a sore thumb. I end up with the clients who believe in innovation and give me the opportunity to do something different. I believe in the need to inject new energy from outside a closed system. When we reshape our environment we have to add this energy. I'm always looking for new sources of energy.

At 62, I feel that I'm just at the beginning of my career. I remember I.M. Pei saying to me that at 60, he was just beginning to fight.

The important thing is the conviction that you have in life. I let my heart guide my hand. Maki says I'm consistent in exploring my passion for things. When I paint, I take advantage of the circumstances. If there's a problem on site, I try to take advantage of it. That's the way I design buildings and plan cities. You turn liabilities into assets.

Panda Habitat, exterior view (1999)
The new Giant Panda Habitat in Ocean Park is related to my love of nature, my interest in cosmology and the evolution of life. Technology is something that we can use to help animals who already co-exist with us.
Interior view: In my design, visitors have to go into the pandas' environment, rather than the animals coming into our environment to entertain us. The temperature is maintained at fifteen to twenty degrees. The humidity is 50%. We also have mist generators and there's running water, which they can bathe in. I insisted that nothing should resemble any human artefact, like a plastic slide or a car tyre. I wanted to do this job so much, I participated physically in the building process. I positioned rocks, planted trees myself on site. It's like creating a living environment, thinking I'm a panda – where do I want to sit? In designing this, I'm not making an architectural statement. The point is not the style, it's the ambiance for the pandas.

The current resurgence of interest in Southeast Asian vernacular styles dignifies the reclaiming of tradition as something that is not merely desirable and tasteful but also as a philosophy that is culturally and somewhat politically correct. The prolific production of text and tomes of seductive images, whether they clarify or fudge the pertinent issues, saw also the proliferation of the *tropical* and *vernacular* styles.

But the agenda that has fuelled the survival of tradition in the past cannot be assumed to hold for the current resurgence. The present reclaiming mindset blends in a yearning for history, a search for identity (in a moment when it's deemed to be in crisis), a romance with nostalgia and a dream of an exotic critical regionalism, the last substantiating the reclaiming work with intellectual ballast.

Additional factors augment this harking back for inspiration and substance. There's for one, the renewed interest in phenomenology which sought to counterbalance the abstract and intellectual bias of Modernism. Sensuousness in architecture is once again seen as important. It's acceptable and desirable to make architecture that evokes the temporal rhythms, invokes the nuances of light and amplifies the textures of materials to stir the senses. To this end, the traditional precedences have a developed vocabulary for architects to borrow easily from.

Then there's the environmental cause. A cause to help conserve limited resources easily lends credence to the low-tech climatic solutions of tropical architecture.

The work of Ernesto Bedmar is set within this milieu. When he completed his first tropical style house at No. 8 Bin Tong Park (1990), the invocation of the vernacular was still a novel thing. That project was meant partly as a reaction against the banal use of PoMo (in ways that would make Michael Graves weep) then. The quotation of vernacular motifs is not unlike PoMo as a device but it can be argued that the borrowing of a Thai *sala* (for example) form has more contextual legitimacy than a rehash of a Greek pediment. Lending real legitimacy to the borrowing of traditional forms and regional precedences is the (re)interpretation and extending of contextual solutions; one of the key contextual issues being climate.

The project generated enough interest to earn a few more commissions. No. 4 Camden Park (1991) came on stream. So did No. 35 Bin Tong Park (1992). This first phase down the traditional route culminated with No. 59A Belmont Road (1992).

These early projects gave opportunities to restage traditional pavillions *and* verandahs; and to rediscover also the tectonics of indigenous Southeast Asian woodframe construction, etc. The beauty of constructional sequences, logic and detail are revealed carefully, especially the roof which is designed to engage the eyes with the whole works – trusses, rafters and all that.

While it seems that there's some degree of romancing the quotations, care was taken to avoid literalness. A modern language, of crisp planes for example, is introduced into the traditional style in as integral a way as possible so as not to degenerate the mix into some wild juxtaposition. Past iconography is also consciously avoided. Found objects may be incorporated but they contribute to decoration and not to the architectural language. The essence was to pare down.

A deeper lesson culled from observations on regional case studies is that of the organic relationship between inside and outside (think of the traditional Thai or Balinese courtyard types which are pavillions arranged in/ around a courtyard). The making of a space syntax that binds intimately internal and external is to become a key theme in Ernesto Bedmar's designs; where the landscape creates a setting for the architecture while the architec-ture creates voids for those little landscaped microcosms. The house is not a mere object in space but delimits outdoor spaces such that there is a controlled variety of framed views, small scale courtyards, expansive vistas... all enriched with water, greenery and sculptural objects.

The design philosophy proved adequate in powering the designs over a series of projects, but the use of tradition seen from the selective lens of the media was construed as giving vigour to traditions without updating them (like viewing traditions through rose-tinted *Raybans*). The price of the Balinese tag implies also a use-by date.

These thoughts brings forth the question – is the *zeitgeist* missing in all these nostalgic excursions into the traditional territory? By extension of that thought, a seemingly more valid questions emerges – **"who is the modern Asian wo(man)?"** In this light, those small incremental steps in paring down the traditional vocabulary to update them seem so conservative.

Ernesto Bedmar

Precedence, Parameters & Change

A key question that has arisen is if there is a more vigorous way of combining tradition with modernity. Is it possible to marry the space syntax of Asian tradition (inside-outside relationships, porosity of the envelope, semi-open intermediate space, etc.) with a modern idiom to speak of an Asian context that can reflect more explicitly the time we are in? Those questions set the direction for current and future projects.

In finding the answers for the new direction, other questions that were asked in the past will continue to be relevant. The question of climate remains a key issue. The view that a building is not a mere shelter but a filter that offers both physical and psychological comfort and pleasures will still be held as an important guide. Architecture according to Ernesto Bedmar will still be regarded as lived-in reality. As such, the manipulation of concrete and abstract phenomena to charge form and space with feelings of poetry, to invoke the notion of balance and harmony will continue to inform future projects. These humanistic parameters will remain fixed even as formal vocabulary, grammar and idiom are experimented upon.

No. 8A Bishopsgate
Singapore, 1997

No. 8A Bishopsgate is designed for the same owner as No. 59A Belmont Road. A key idea used in the latter, which is the gathering of the main spaces to define a water body as the hub of the house, is reprised at Bishopsgate. This water body, like its predecessor, functions both as a reflective pool and a swimming pool.

The similarity, however, ends there. In fact, this house represents a departure from the traditional idioms that BSD has come to be identified with.

Here, roofs are pitched but they go in a mono rather than a double pitch. The roofs are clasped on three sides by crisp white walls with the fourth side left open but infilled with glass. From some angles, the composition of walls (which conceal the roofs) read as modernist boxes. It is intended that the reading of the house shifts as different angles are viewed. The design represents a point of balance between derivations from the modern and the traditional.

An internally orientated house, a timber deck contained by an enormous pierced concrete wall draws a veil across the intrusive windows of a neighbouring house.

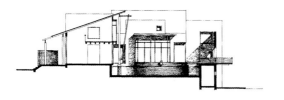

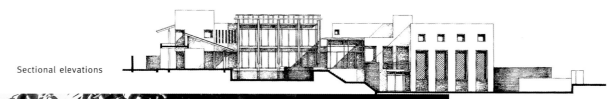

Sectional elevations

But like other Ernesto Bedmar's projects, concrete and abstract phenomena are composed to make an architecture that has a rich sensory dimension. Despite the change in the architectural language, there still remains the tactile, visual and experiential variety. There's a deliberate attempt to balance the rough and the smooth in what you see and what you walk on. The change to reflect on the play of light and shadow on water is also present.

It is fortuitous that that site is an awkward pie-shape, with the narrow neck in front. The opportunity to create an architectural promenade was seized. In fact, the shape of the site lent a legitimacy to the use of the circuitous device; which traces out a route that takes you on a little journey to discover a variety of spaces, vistas and objects.

The huge existing Angsana tree which has, with some difficulty, been retained.

Entering the main door one can appreciate the pool and the steel columns supporting the living room pavilion.

The rear courtyard is a place of solitude shaded by a screen of mature trees.

Second storey plan

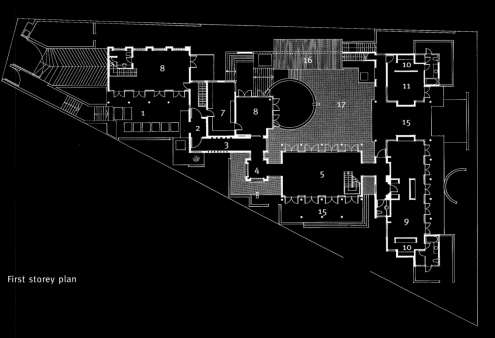

First storey plan

1   Entry courtyard
2   Entrance
3   Corridor
4   Hall
5   Living room
6   Dining room
7   Kitchen
8   Studio en suite
9   Master bedroom
10 Dressing room
11 Guest room
12 Bedroom
13 Terrace
14 Family Hall
15 Covered terrace
16 Pool deck
17 Swimming pool
18 Garage
19 Entrance from garage
20 Laundry room
21 Asian kitchen
22 Maid's room
23 Wine cellar
24 Store

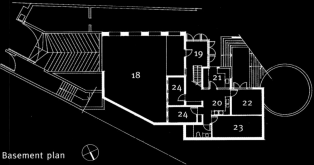

Basement plan

Residence 8 Development
Singapore, 1999

The brief for the strata-title cluster housing development called for 8 semi-detached units (with communal facilities and a full basement with car parking) to be fitted into a small site of about 2546 sq m. The demands on a speculative housing design are adhered to. Set-backs are pushed to the minimum allowable so that the highest allowable plot ratio can be achieved. There's no space for sprawl, thus making an urban approach to the planning of the development somewhat not an option but a necessity. To that end, the houses are strung out along a street.

As a result of the intense site usage which pushed the eight units almost into a cheek-by-jowl fit, the question of privacy for each unit arose as a key issue. Also, given the tight fit, the question of orienting external views from the inside of the units to give the illusion of a spacious outdoor extension became important.

View of main unit facade from main circulation.

Close up view of roof and volumes defining different internal spaces.

Sectional elevations

Other design decisions include the flipping of the living rooms to the rear where they have direct access to the rear garden. The side-to-side set-back between units are excavated almost to their full extent into the basement level so as to bring in as much light and air as possible into the guest and family rooms located below. A garden and pond are provided next to these rooms. And also, every unit has a roof deck.

The lightness of the modern architectural language, with projecting lanterns, floating 'butterfly' roofs, curtain walls, dissolved corners, not only aids in bringing more light into the interior but also gives a soaring and expansive character to the internal spaces. It is intended that the tight fit of the eight units within a small site ibe not apparent when within the houses.

Detail of balcony and rainwater downpipe.

Rear view of unit showing different treatment and language.

Second storey plan

A Rubbish bin	11 Access to unit
B Substation	12 Lobby
C Electrical room	13 Living room
1 Vehicular entrance	14 Dining room
2 Pedestrian entrance	15 Kitchen
3 Main circulation	16 Service yard
4 Swimming pool	17 Maid's room
5 Pool deck	18 Family room
6 Access to basement	19 Guest bedroom
7 Car park	20 Courtyard
8 Access to units	21 Master bedroom
9 Changing room	22 Bedroom
10 Technical room	

Internal view of unit circulation

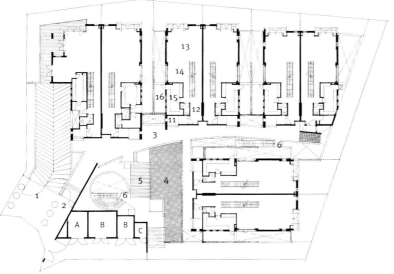

First storey plan

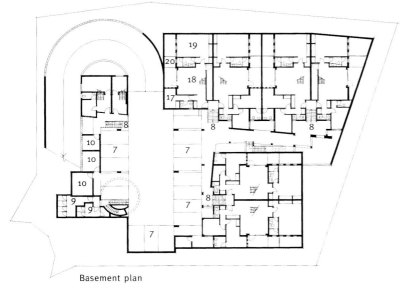

Basement plan

House in Singapore
Singapore. 2000.

Site & Planning Concepts

Except for a steep 3 m slope, the site located in the suburbs of Singapore, is generally flat. The topography is perfect for tucking a basement for the house in such a way that the basement projects out into the open at the slope end to allow natural light and ventilation into the rooms there. It is also opportune that the slope occurs two-thirds of the way into the length of the site from the chosen arrival point for the house; the arrival point (via a cul-de-sac at the rear) sits on the higher platform level. The bulk of the house is located on this higher platform level allowing it to command a vantage view of the generous greenery that surrounds the site.

The accommodation is organised into two main blocks. Both are two-storey pavilion style blocks lined up parallel to the east and west boundaries respectively. The block adjacent to the west boundary features the basement and a dining room pavilion, the latter nudged partly into the pavilion block. Designed as a concrete flat roof structure, the dining room also projects into the adjacent swimming pool to simulate a "floating" effect. Both pavilion

Vista of garden from the main entrance.

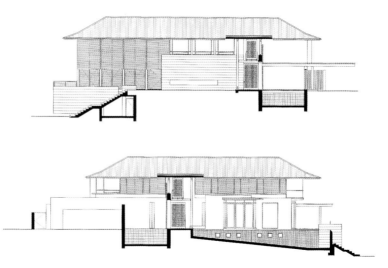

View of the porous outdoor living room. The panels of timber battens, allow light and natural ventilation to filter into the indoor space.

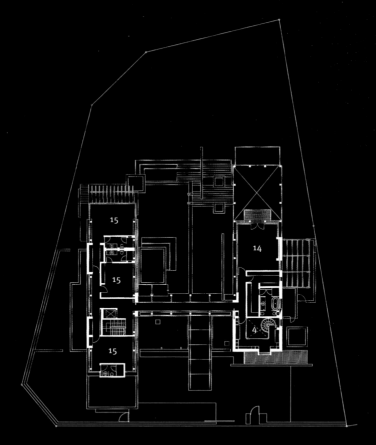

Second floor plan

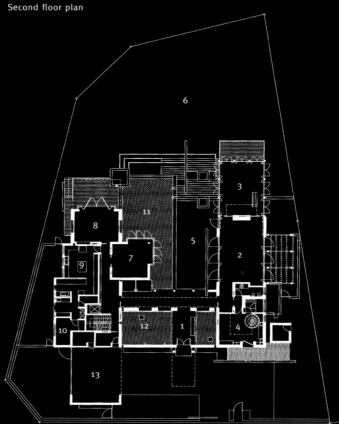

1   Entry bridge
2   Living room
3   Outdoor living room
4   Study
5   Upper garden
6   Lower garden
7   Dining room
8   TV room
9   Kitchen
10 Maid's room
11 Swimming pool
12 Fish pond
13 Garage
14 Master bedroom
15 Bedrooms

First floor plan

blocks point in the north-south axis. But their long exposures along the east and west boundaries, which are most susceptible to heat gain, are amply shaded by existing trees. Care and caution were taken to retain the trees during the construction of the house.

The two-block schema is not meant as a straightforward and literal means of separating private and public zones. Rather, rooms from both categories are integrated for more interesting adjacency relationships. One example of this adjacency is the co-locating of the master bedroom and the living room such that the former commands a view of the latter from a high point.

Landscaping

Connecting the two pavilion blocks is a corridor-bridge, roofed over but open at the sides. A feature pond flanks the corridor-bridge on the side adjacent to the main entrance. The pond, shielded completely from the carporch by an inscrutable granite wall is experienced only once past the threshold of the main door.

As an arrival element, the pond is also the first in the series of landscape features that pushes out directionally from the main entrance door. Beyond the pond and the frame of the corridor-bridge, the interstice between the

View of the corridor-bridge from the end of swimming pool.

Detail of water spout.

pavilion blocks is filled with the swimming pool and a lawn running alongside it. This longitudinal push of the landscape finds a transition at the slope. There the pool spills over a sharp edge to tumble down a 2 m tall stone wall while the lawn cascades as a set of solid granite garden steps that lead to the lower level garden below. The garden below departs from the pristine character of the lawn and takes on a "wild" quality.

The directional push of the landscape directs the eye to the far view from the entrance point. This visual direction predominantly emphasised by the two pavilion blocks is augmented with two granite planes. One granite plane, with a cutout slot, acts as a screen for the living room; while the other slices into the cascade of granite garden steps, its free end lifted off the ground as the latter continues to slope away.

The landscape design is integral to the visual and experiential aspects of the architecture. Greenery and water features fill the spaces between the building blocks. There is a view of water from every room (of either feature pond or swimming pool). Movement between the two blocks via the open corridor-bridge takes one past the landscape. A timber deck that hovers over the lower garden extends the living room into an outdoor space where one can command a vantage view of the greenery below. The living room features also an outdoor patio shaded by a trellis while the games room has an outdoor terrace sheltered by a pergola.

Corridor-bridge looking in the direction of the door to the living room.

View of the cascade of garden steps that lead from the lawn to the lower garden.

The emphasis put on the landscape design and the integration of the landscape with the architecture are attempts at appreciating the meaning of living in the tropics. Air movement, passive cooling, a sense of closeness with nature and greenery (which living in the tropics allow all year round), etc. are determinants of the architectural design.

Architecture

The traditional Southeast Asian pavilion is the inspiration for the architectural form and idiom of the house. However, the precedence is updated both in terms of its style and tectonics though not just for aesthetic effect. Rather, the update responds to various issues such as the need for more privacy (the house cannot be as porous as the traditional pavilion), the use of current construction materials and techniques and the programmatic differences between a traditional pavilion and a contemporary house.

Internal view of the indoor living room. The room enjoys good connection with the outdoor.

Throughout human history, the sky has carried a profound and sacred meaning. Man intuitively perceived it as the abode of the Supernatural. Hence to climb a path to the top of the hill, where the gods dwell, is a paradigm of such mythic power that it has been central to the beliefs of almost every society since the beginning of time.

Thus the great Hindu temples of South India are not just a collection of shrines and gopurams, but a movement through the open-to-sky pathways that lie between them. Such a path is the essence of our experience – it represents a sacred journey, a ritualistic pathway, a pradakshina, a pilgrimage. And this sense of the sky extends to the architectonic vocabulary as well: as witness the walls around Rajasthan palaces and Moghul forts, crowned with patterns that interlock: built form with sky – and the wonderfully evocative chattris (umbrellas) along the roofscape, capturing fragments of the infinite heavens above.

In India the sky has profoundly affected our relationship to built form and to open space. For in a warm climate, the best place to be in the late evening and in the early morning is outdoors, under the open sky. Such spaces have an infinite number of variations: one steps out of a room... into a verandah... and thence onto a terrace... from which one proceeds to an open courtyard, perhaps shaded by a tree... or by a large pergola overhead. At each moment, subtle changes in the quality of light and ambient air generate feelings within – feelings which are central to our beings. Hence to us in Asia, the symbol of Education has never been the Little Red Schoolhouse of North America, but the guru sitting under the tree. True Enlightenment cannot be achieved within the closed box of a room – one must be outdoors, under the open sky.

These open-to-sky spaces have very practical implications as well. To the poor in their cramped dwellings, the roof terrace and the courtyard represent an additional room, used in many different ways during the course of a day: for cooking, for talking to friends, for sleeping at night, and so forth. And for the rich, at the other end of the income spectrum, the lawn is as precious as the bungalow itself. Thus in traditional villages and towns all over India, such open-to-sky spaces are an essential element in the lives of the people.

The blessings of the sky are truly munificent – and here we will seek to examine two of the most crucial.

The first looks at Housing – where the crusial importance of open-to-sky space in the warm climates of the Third World. The Cablenager

Open-to-Sky Spaces

Township (1967) in the
hot dry desert around
Kota, in Rajasthan – a
project that was not built,
but which was of seminal
importance to the various
housing typologies we
developed in succeeding
decades. The concept of
this township was itself
triggered off by the Tube
House (1962), a design
which won first prize in
the all-India low-cost
housing competition
organised by the Gujarat
Housing Board. Here the
profile of the house was
arranged so that hot air,
rising and moving along
the sloping surfaces of
the ceiling, could escape
from a vent at the apex,
thus drawing in replace-
ments of cooler air from
the lower levels. In
Cablenagar, this principle
is further developed to
generate a whole range
of house types, of
carrying floor areas and
spatial configurations, for
different categories of
company staff.

From the housing for
Cablenagar grew the
Parekh House (1968) in
Ahmedabad, which uses
two pyramidal sections.
The Summer Section

(usable in the hot dry season and on winter evenings)
closes off the heat from the sky. Conversely, the
Winter Section (usable in the cold season and on the
summer evenings), inverts the pyramid, opening up
the terraces to the sky. Since the site for the Parekh
House is east-west, the Summer Section is sand-
wiched between the Winter Section on one side and a
service bay on the other.

These examples are in hot-dry regions of India, but
how this approach can be made viable in hot-humid
context (where cross-ventilation is of crucial importance) is illustrated by the Kanchanjunga (1970-83), a
condominium of luxury apartments located in a high-
rise residential section of Bombay. In this building
designed for the hot-humid climate, the units inter-

lock so as to form
double-height terrace
gardens which protect the
inhabitants from the sun
and rain, in an analogue
of the verandahs found in
traditional bungalows.
These terraces, located at
the corners of the plan,
are cantilevered over the
city, opening up spectacular views of the harbour
on one side and the
Arabian Sea on the other
– giving back to the
inhabitants of this very
dense section of the city
the blessings of the sky.

The second theme, the
importance of open-to-
sky spaces to the Public
realm, is illustrated by
two projects which are
also vehicles for
exploring vital issues in
India today. The proces-
sional unfolding of
spaces, some enclosed,
some open-to-sky,
developed in Bharat
Bhavan (1975-81), Bhopal
– which is a reinterpreta-
tion of the old Pleasure
Gardens which are still a
popular spot for families
in the cool hours of
sunset and in the early
dawn. In the JNIDB in
Hyderabad (1986-91), the
pathway moves like a

river through the build-
ing, connecting the
teaching areas to the
library and faculty offices,
and up to the hostel
rooms on the sloping
site, while in the National
Crafts Museum (1975-85),
it becomes a continuous
pedestrian spine running
through the heart of the
museum – a metaphor for
the Indian street, taking
the visitor from village to
temple to palace.

In the second project
illustrated here the British
Council Headquarters and
Library in Delhi (1987-92),
this pathway becomes a
formal axis, running down
the centre of the site,
from the entrance gate
right up to the rear
boundary. Along it are
three mythic paradigms
that have generated the
history of this subconti-
nent, recalling the historic
interfaces that have
existed between India
and England over the
centuries. At the end is
the oldest one: the
interface with Hinduism,
symbolised by the
ancient Vedic Bindu (the
source of all energy). In
the middle is the inter-
face with Islam, repre-

sented by the Char Bagh (the Koranic Garden of
Paradise). The third *axis mundi*, brought by the English
who arrived with their own mythic beliefs in Science
and Rationality, is a traditional European one (precisely
the same as used by Lutyens in his Viceroy's House in
New Delhi). Presiding over the entrance to all of this is
an extraordinary mural by Howard Hodgkin, symbolising the shade of a giant banyan tree.

Large square cut-outs on the street facade not only
encase the Hodgkin mural like a proscenium but also,
from within the building, act as "urban windows"
framing views of the city outside – a visual and gesture
that recalls the double-height terraces of Kanchanjunga, suspended high above Bombay, which act as
"urban windows" framing the city.

The third project is the
Vidhan Bhavan, a highly
complex interlock of
pathways, built form
and open-to-sky spaces
for the new State
Assembly for the
Government of Madhya
Pradesh (1980-96).
Here there are several
different pathways,
each independent of the
others – and yet each
one formal and ritualis-
tic. Thus every one of
the various users
(ministers, politicians,
VIPs, visiting peasants,
the press, etc.) can,
from their own pathway,
experience the main
vistas and monumental
spaces of this complex.
It is a citadel of
democracy – built in
circular form.

The plan of the Vidhan
Bhavan was an outcome
of the nature of the site
(on the top of a hill in
the middle of Bhopal),
as well as its proximity
to the stupa at Sanchi –
an overwhelmingly
powerful three-dimen-
sional representation of
the ancient Buddhist
cosmography (sacred
diagrams depicting the
entire manifest world).

British Council
Delhi, 1987-92.

This new building for the British Council houses a number of diverse functions, including a library, an auditorium, an art gallery and the headquarters of their offices in India. These elements are arranged in a series of layers, recalling the historic interfaces that have existed between India and Britain over the last several centuries. From the main entrance gate, one moves down the main axis which extends right up to the rear garden wall. The three nodal points along this axis are structured around three *axes mundi,* each recalling one of the principal belief systems that exist in the Indian sub-continent. At the farthest end is the *axis mundi* of Hinduism, a spiral symbolising Bindu – the energy centre of the Cosmos. The next nodal point, located in the main courtyard is centred around another mythic image: the traditional Islamic Char Bagh (Garden of Paradise). The third nodal point along this axis is a European icon inlaid in marble and granite used to represent the Age of Reason including the mythic values of Science and Progress.

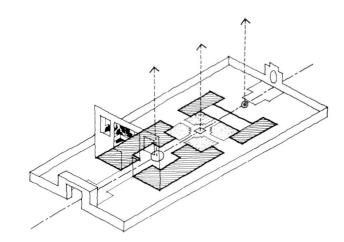

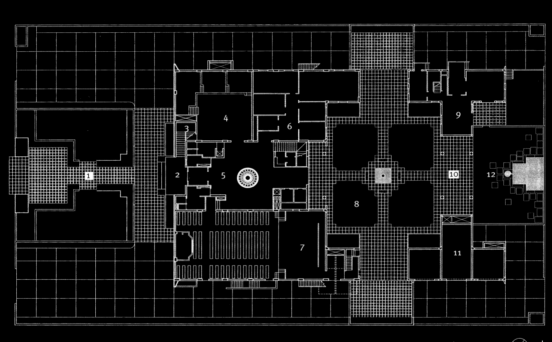

Site Plan

1 Entrance court
2 Main entrance
3 To library
4 Exhibition gallery
5 Foyer
6 Meeting rooms
7 Auditorium
8 Char Bagh
9 Residence
10 Loggia
11 Maintenance
12 Bindu

0   10m

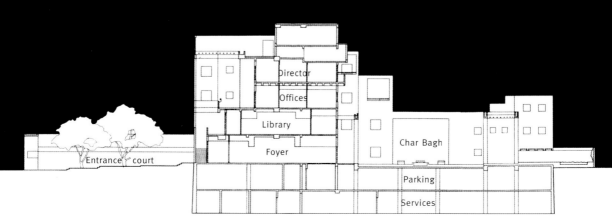

Director

Offices

Library

Foyer

Entrance court

Char Bagh

Parking

Services

A double-height terrace.

Kanchanjunga Apartments
Bombay. 1970-83.

In Bombay a building has to be oriented east-west to catch the prevailing sea-breezes and to open up the best views in the city: the Arabian Sea on one side and the harbour on the other. But these unfortunately are also the directions of the hot sun and the heavy monsoon rains. The old bungalows solved these problems by wrapping a protective layer of verandahs around the main living areas thus providing the occupants with two lines of defence against the elements. Kanchanjunga, an attempt to apply these principles to a high-rise building, is a condominium of 32 luxury apartments of four different types, varying from three to six bedrooms each. The interlock of these variations is expressed externally by the shear end walls that hold up the cantilevers. The tower has a proportion of 1:4 (being 21 metres square and 84 metres high). Its minimalist unbroken surfaces are cut away to open up the double-height terrace gardens at the corners, thus revealing (through the interlocking form and colour) some hint of the complex spatial organisation of living spaces that lie within the tower.

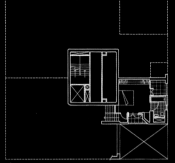

Three bedroom unit: upper level

Three bedroom unit: entrance level

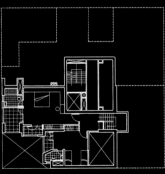

Four bedroom unit: upper level

Four bedroom unit: entrance level

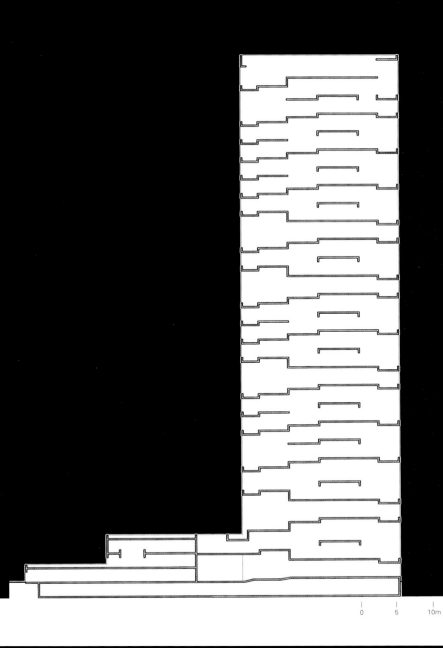

0	5	10m

The stupa at Sanchi to which the
Vidhan Bhavan alludes.

Vidhan Bhavan, State Assembly
Bhopal, 1980-96.

The new Vidhan Bhavan State Assembly Complex has been built to accommodate many of the diverse functions crucial to a functioning democracy. Besides the Vidhan Sabha (for 366 members) and the Vidhan Parishad (which will house 75 members), there are suites of offices for the Speaker of the House, for the Chief Minister, for the Chief Secretary and their supporting staff. In addition, there are 70 offices for ministers and their personal assistants, together with committee rooms and section offices.

The large murals, sculpture, paintings and artwork found throughout the building are vivid examples of the great artistic traditions of the State – from the magnificent murals covering the walls around the kund (painted by the finest folk artists of Bastar), to the green-marbled sculpture of the Goddess of the Narmada River floating above the reflecting pool, to the many exquisite art objects in the offices and along public verandahs. Situated on the crest of a hill in the centre of Bhopal, the building affords magnificent views of the city all around. Truly it is a celebration of the State of Madhya Pradesh, of its culture and its people – a veritable Palace of Democracy.

The plan generates a pattern of gardens within gardens divided into 9 squares. The five central ones (along the two main axes) are halls and courtyards while the four corner positions are occupied by specialised functions: the Vidhan Sabha (Lower House), the Vidhan Parishad (Upper House), the Combined Hall, and the Library.

There are three main entrances: for the public, for the Speaker (the VIP Entrance), and for the MLAs. The plan is arranged so that these three streams, each quite separate from the others, experience the complex internal spaces of the building while moving along verandahs overlooking courtyards and gardens, as in the traditional architecture of India.

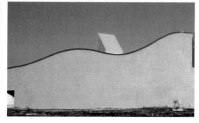

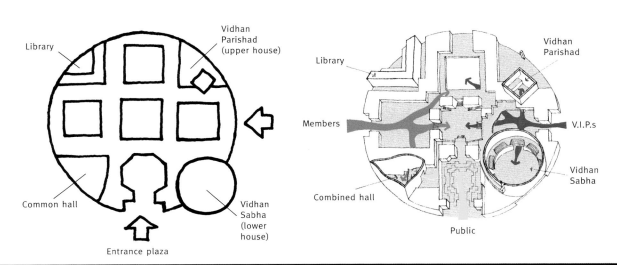

Library

Vidhan
Parishad
(upper house)

Common hall

Vidhan
Sabha
(lower
house)

Entrance plaza

Library

Members

Combined hall

Vidhan
Parishad

V.I.P.s

Vidhan
Sabha

Public

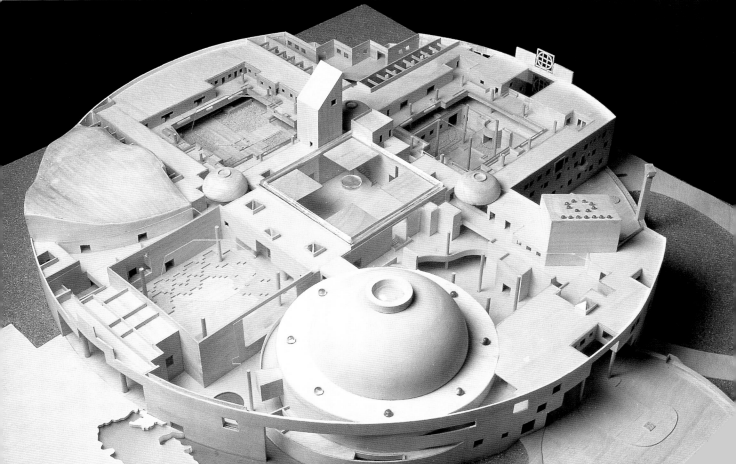

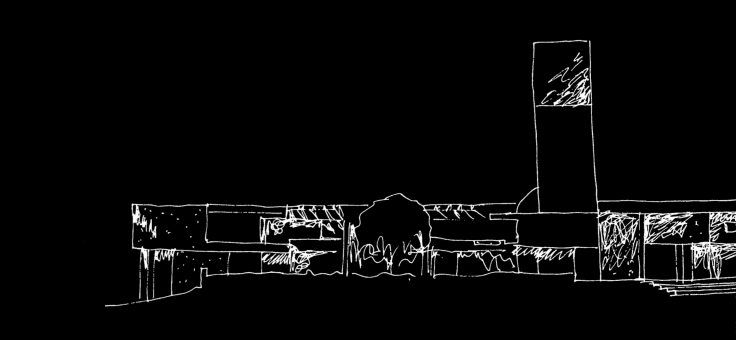

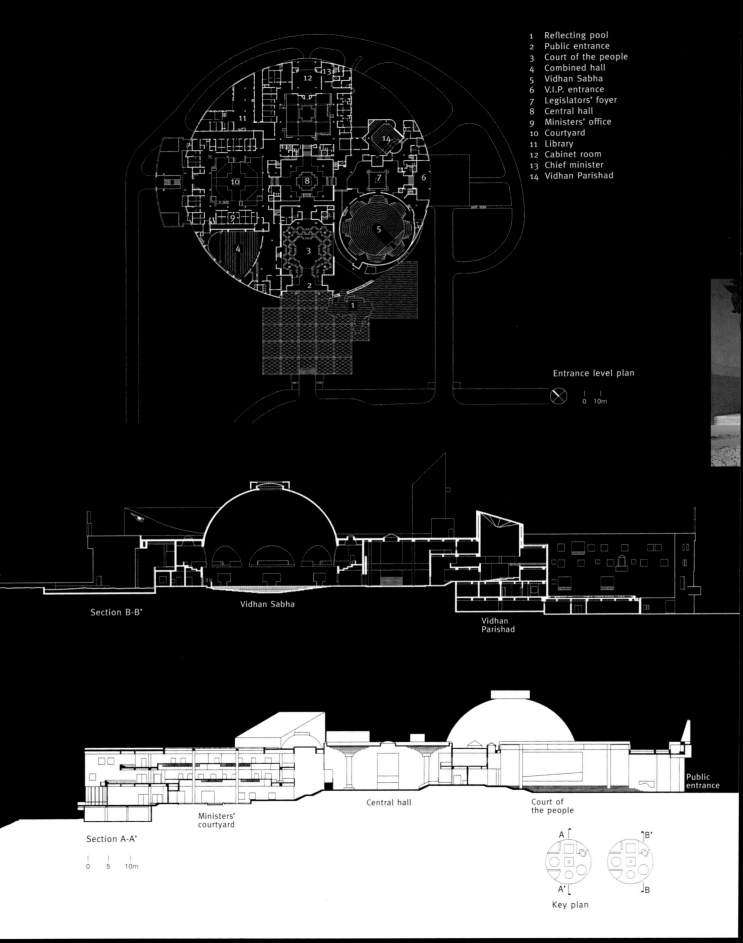

1 Reflecting pool
2 Public entrance
3 Court of the people
4 Combined hall
5 Vidhan Sabha
6 V.I.P. entrance
7 Legislators' foyer
8 Central hall
9 Ministers' office
10 Courtyard
11 Library
12 Cabinet room
13 Chief minister
14 Vidhan Parishad

Entrance level plan

0   10m

Section B-B'

Vidhan Sabha

Vidhan
Parishad

Section A-A'

0   5   10m

Ministers'
courtyard

Central hall

Court of
the people

Public
entrance

A   B'

A'   B

Key plan

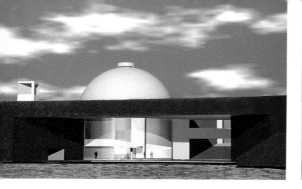
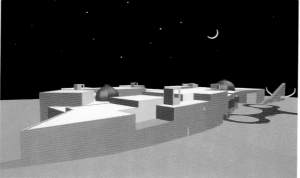

Museum of Islamic Arts
Doha, Qatar, 1997.

The programme of the Museum of Islamic Arts was formulated by the Aga Khan Trust for Culture. Eight international architects were shortlisted for a competition, which was judged by an international jury consisting of Ricardo Legoretta, Fumihiko Maki, Luis Monreal and others. This museum will display to the public the paintings, weaponry, glassware, numismatics, books and manuscripts of the collection of Al-Thani family of the State of Qatar.

In a museum of Islamic art, the nature of the object on display takes on a particular significance. The primary issue is to place and illuminate objects in sequence – so that they communicate with a moving observer. OBJECT, ROUTE and LIGHT thus become the basic elements of design. The distinction between secular and religious art, so strong in the west, is non-existent and highly blurred in this culture. So also is the difference between the artist and the craftsman. All makers are artist-craftsmen; for them, life and art are whole. A museum of Islamic art must express these special values through its architecture.

In this museum, the programme consists of a number of various-sized galleries linked along a continuous path. The galleries are flexible and autonomous. The pathways offer several alternative routes for visitors to view the exhibition areas in a variety of sequences. A sense of centrality is provided by assembling the galleries around the central courtyard. The plan is designed around two central themes: a central courtyard and an undulating wall. Although it is a simple design, it boldly communicates the presence of a strong and vibrant cultural institution.

The main façade, an undulating wall, has a symbolic quality that gives the building a strong identity when viewed from the Corniche. Through this design, an architectural element, the wall, is used to make a bold and poignant "urban gesture". In this interpretation of the wall, polished red granite is used to mirror the sea and the sky, and is modulated in thickness and height along its length. The resulting curves serve both form and function, as they contain different service spaces used by the galleries, such as cargo elevators and access to storage facilities.

The wall terminates in the form of a triangular astronomical instrument, making a tribute and reference to the achievements of Islam in science and astronomy. The wall can be reached from the didactic collection or directly from the entrance plaza, also serving the public as a platform to overlook the Corniche and the city of Doha.

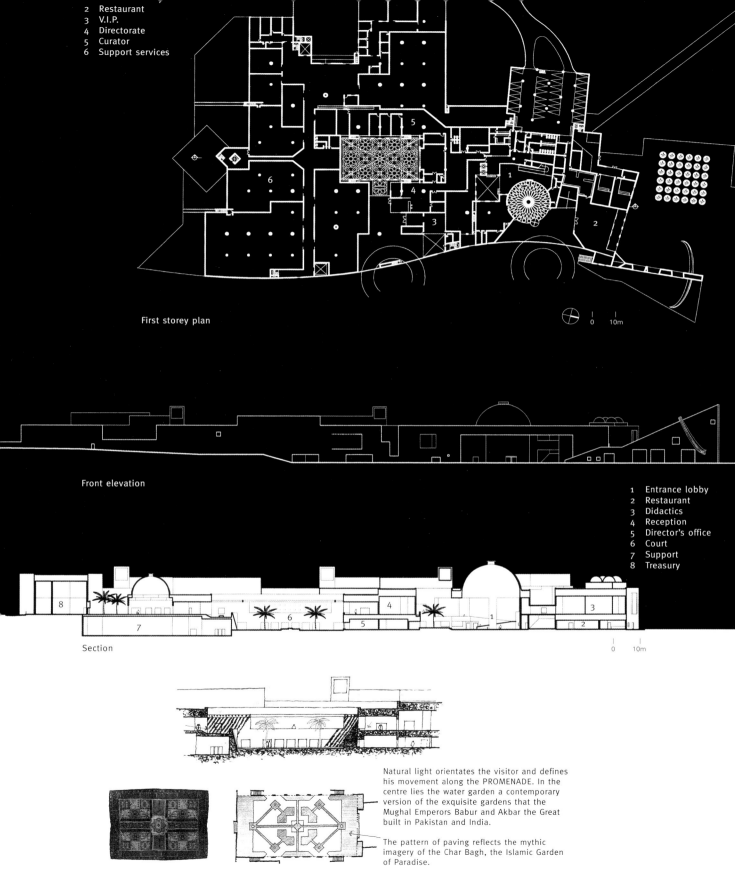

2 Restaurant
3 V.I.P.
4 Directorate
5 Curator
6 Support services

First storey plan

$\begin{array}{ccc} & | & | \\ 0 & & 10m \end{array}$

Front elevation

1 Entrance lobby
2 Restaurant
3 Didactics
4 Reception
5 Director's office
6 Court
7 Support
8 Treasury

Section

$\begin{array}{ccc} | & & | \\ 0 & & 10m \end{array}$

Natural light orientates the visitor and defines his movement along the PROMENADE. In the centre lies the water garden a contemporary version of the exquisite gardens that the Mughal Emperors Babur and Akbar the Great built in Pakistan and India.

The pattern of paving reflects the mythic imagery of the Char Bagh, the Islamic Garden of Paradise.

121

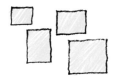

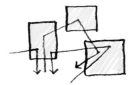

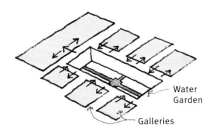

Water
Garden

Galleries

The program of this museum calls for a number of various-sized galleries – each one a vital link in a continuous sequence. At the same time, each gallery should be flexible and autonomous

Then again, the path along which the visitor travels should offer several alternatives, so that the galleries can be viewed in various sequences (or, indeed, some of them skipped altogether) – thus allowing each new visit to the muesum to become a fresh and vivid experience.

By assembling the different-sized galleries around a central courtyard, we not only can optimise the options available to the visitor, but also create something very fundamental to the architecture of Islam: CENTRALITY. This courtyard is a water garden – which not only serves to humidify the dry desert air, but acts as a metaphor for that timeless desert gathering place: the oasis.

The primary route which goes from the entrance to the promenade around a central courtyard is daylit – and becomes a Line of Light, binding the various elements of the museum together.

In the centre, the mythic image to which one returns again and again: the Garden of Paradise.

From this promenade, each of the galleries can be entered separately. A visitor can therefore decide what to see and each gallery can have its own character, yet be a part of a coherent and understandable whole.

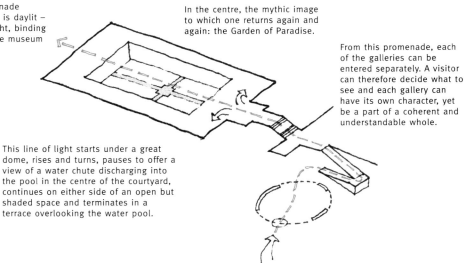

This line of light starts under a great dome, rises and turns, pauses to offer a view of a water chute discharging into the pool in the centre of the courtyard, continues on either side of an open but shaded space and terminates in a terrace overlooking the water pool.

Transition passages: between galleries, narrow spaces with large images and texts introduce the gallery spaces to come.

Framing objects in columns of light: minimal lights on suspended almost invisible structures hold objects, coins, etc. Enlargements to full wall height of images in macro photography are as sharp as new technology can make them.

Textures: in the gallery the walls might be covered and richly textured perhaps in fabrics, or other materials.

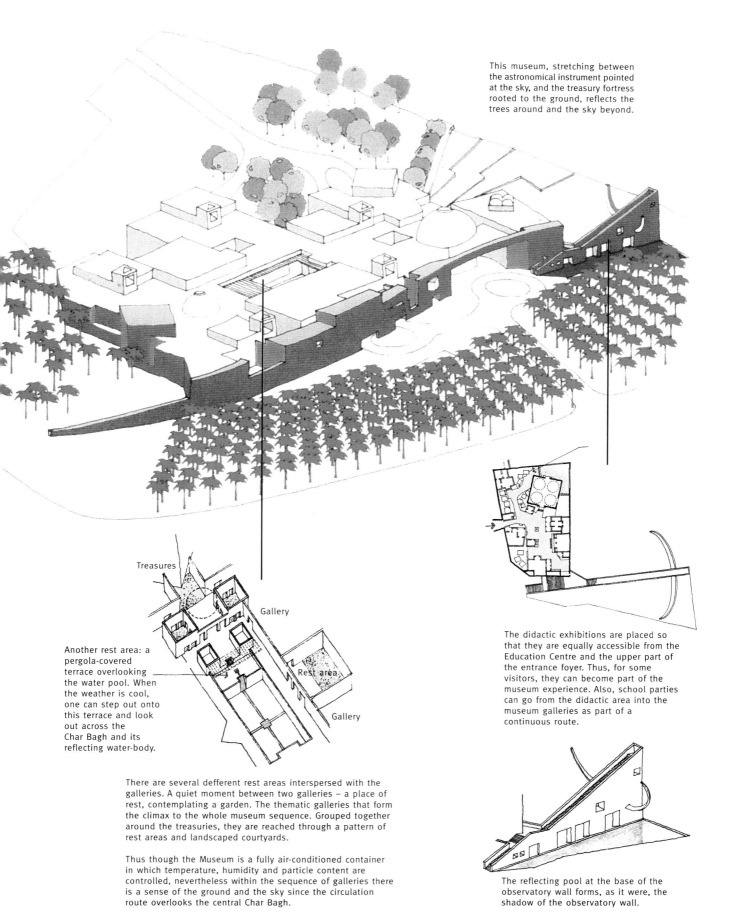

This museum, stretching between the astronomical instrument pointed at the sky, and the treasury fortress rooted to the ground, reflects the trees around and the sky beyond.

Treasures

Gallery

Rest area

Gallery

Another rest area: a pergola-covered terrace overlooking the water pool. When the weather is cool, one can step out onto this terrace and look out across the Char Bagh and its reflecting water-body.

There are several defferent rest areas interspersed with the galleries. A quiet moment between two galleries – a place of rest, contemplating a garden. The thematic galleries that form the climax to the whole museum sequence. Grouped together around the treasuries, they are reached through a pattern of rest areas and landscaped courtyards.

Thus though the Museum is a fully air-conditioned container in which temperature, humidity and particle content are controlled, nevertheless within the sequence of galleries there is a sense of the ground and the sky since the circulation route overlooks the central Char Bagh.

The didactic exhibitions are placed so that they are equally accessible from the Education Centre and the upper part of the entrance foyer. Thus, for some visitors, they can become part of the museum experience. Also, school parties can go from the didactic area into the museum galleries as part of a continuous route.

The reflecting pool at the base of the observatory wall forms, as it were, the shadow of the observatory wall.

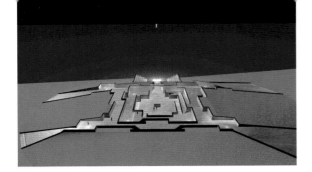

Buddhapurnima Lakefront Development
Hyderabad. 1998 to date.

Hyderabad is an historic city in South India, whose principal image is the Charminar – a gateway built in the 16th century and located in the oldest and the densest part of the city. Hyderabad is striving to be India's most dynamic and progressive city. High profile projects like the Hitech City, the proposed state-of-the-art Airport, and other concerted efforts to improve the environment have now placed the city on the international map. To substantiate this progressive image of the Hyderabad City, the Buddhapurnima Lakefront can be developed as an icon for the city.

The lake is located at the conurbation of Hyderabad, Secunderabad and Begumpet. In order to develop the lake into this iconic image, we analysed it holistically – so that with all its new facilities, the lake will be the focus of the city. Each component on the available sites is to be developed to its full potential. Along with the Government we have identified 21 sites, which have the potential to be developed for the various purposes.

The Periphery of the Lake:
Along the eastern edge of the lake, runs Tank Bund Road – a busy thoroughfare connecting Hyderabad and Secunderabad. To the west and north is the sweep of Necklace Road, a new road that has been built by HUDA along the edge of the lake, opening up land to the public, which was not previously accessible due to earlier encroachments. This land, between Necklace Road and the lake is ZONE 1 and is earmarked for outdoor public facilities – such as entertainment, food, recreation and culture.

Since Hyderabad's rapid growth over the last years has not been matched by a corresponding increase in its public spaces, the lake and its environs have the potential and the size to fit this role – a public plaza for the city's people and a symbol for the city. The land between Necklace Road and the railway line is ZONE 2 and is earmarked for other facilities for the city, which require built-form, such as a convention centre, a museum, an amusement park, etc.

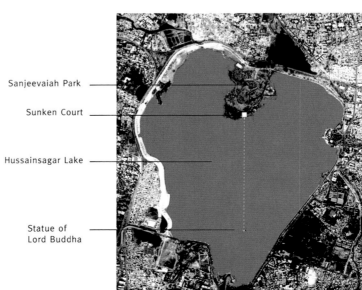

Sanjeevaiah Park

Sunken Court

Hussainsagar Lake

Statue of
Lord Buddha

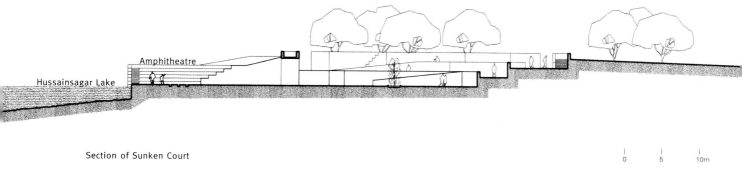

Section of Sunken Court

0	5	10m

Circulation and Transport network:

The circulation and transport network around the lake is to be developed so that it is easily accessible to the people of Hyderabad. Presently, the principal means to reach Necklace Road is by private transport. This limits its visitors to only the upper income group and parking facilities have to be provided, thereby using up large areas of prime land. Public transport is therefore essential – as it will dramatically increase the number of visitors, especially the middle and lower classes.

The network of new jetties will ensure connections at various points without having to travel by land. Jetties will be provided at the food courts and Sanjeevaiah Park, while the existing ones near the Sailing Club, Lumbini Park and the Statue of Buddha will be improved. With these connections, one could spend an entire day without travelling by land, which could be a totally different experience in the city.

We have designed in detail the food courts, the promenade, whose construction has started along Necklace Road, and the Sunken Court – a small cultural centre on the edge of the Hussainsagar Lake in Sanjeevaiah Park.

Sunken Court:

The axis between the Sanjeevaiah Park and the Buddha statue in the lake aligns with the cardinal North-South direction. The Sunken Court is located on this axis to have visual connection with the statue. The Court is an amorphous "non-building" with sides covered by green mounds. One descends towards the centre down ramps and steps to finally culminate in an open-air amphitheatre, overlooking the lake. A reflecting pool in the centre connects the Sunken Court to the lake beyond.

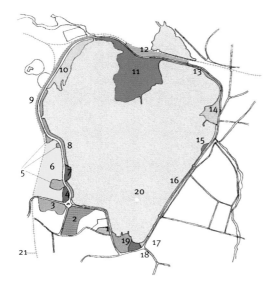

Along with the government we have identified 21 sites which have potential and could be developed:

1 Secretariat extension
2 NTR garden
3 South of Khairatabad Flyover
4 Wetlands
5 Miscellaneous pockets
6 Mader-Saheb-ka-Maktha
7 Exhibition grounds
8 Land between Necklace Road and Lake
9 Land between Railway and Necklace Road
10 Rock garden
11 Sanjeevaiah Park
12 Land in front of Sanjeevaiah Park
13 Land between road and lake
14 Land adjacent to Sailing Club
15 Rotary Park
16 Tank Bund Road
17 Sagar Park
18 Fisheries site
19 Lumbini Park
20 Statue of Lord Buddha
21 Railway line

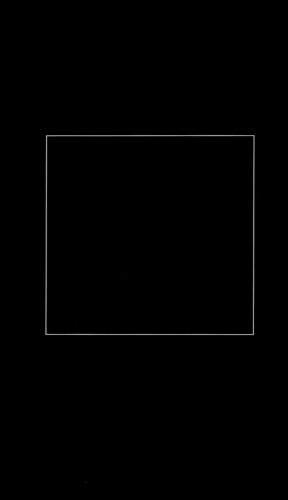

Seung H. Sang

Beauty of Poverty

Cultural complex, 'munwhagonggan', 1994.

In Seoul, the tragic collapse of both the Seongsoo Grand Bridge (proud of its short construction time) in 1994 and Sampo-ong Shopping Center (a symbol of overnight millionaires) in 1995, having taken more than 600 lives, were not regarded as accidents caused just by the structural and technical problems in construction. As for me, it indicated the breakdown of logic that has sustained modern Korean society – a single minded pursuit of wealth in the last decades without knowing why.

Landscapes of cities and suburbs of Korea at the beginning of the 21st century do not seem to have had a history of five thousand years, traces of them are hard to find. We can excuse ourselves by saying that there was the Japanese colonial occupation and the tragic Korean War which practically devastated the foundation of our society and culture. If only we had not lost the core of it, we might have managed to create a new history and cultivate a splendid culture and eventually nurture an environment for a refined contemporary architecture.

But what we see now is a Seoul with no identity but polluted with buildings of deceit, empty shells that are superficial and vulgar. Where are we and where are we headed? This is the crisis of our time and a threat to the future. In a well-organised society there is a Zeitgeist that leads and holds it. If this spirit loosens up, with its centre lost, fragments prevalent, society would face the end of an era.

Here I am reminded that the Sun bi spirit, based on voluntary poverty that had kept Chosun Dynasty for 500 years, has perished. And I notice tension and suspense through fragility and feebleness rather than thickness and strength as in the works of Alberto Giacometti, Luis Barragan and Korean painter Soohwa. I could find the possible exit, an escape from the limits and the labyrinth that contemporary architecture is confronted with. Let me call this "Beauty of Poverty".

Here, to 'use' is more important than to 'have', to 'share' more important than to 'add', to 'empty' more important than to 'fill'. Basically, to realise the substantial question, four strategies could be thought out.

Youngdong jail women's hospital, 1993.

Architecture within City, City within Architecture   When both urban environment and architecture stand open to each other, the matrix of life shall not be interrupted. Demolishing the walls which had been there for territory's sake, opening up the left-over space to the rest of the city, extending the urban street into the site – these are the first stages to open life towards the urban environment.

Disfunction   The realisation of 'functional architecture' that we've been forced to learn could result in 'functional life'; but is that really valuable? Let's redefine what we mean by the 'functional': adequately uncomfortable, distant but just enough to walk. This kind of dwellings is healthier. Disfunctional architecture will lead us towards the more functional in its own terms.

Space of Purposelessness   In general, especially in Western architecture, one of the important aims in architecture is to obtain useful space with purpose. However, a space which is just purposeless enough and hard to name as such, would lengthen the life-span of architecture, enable our life to a wider diversity. Madang, the courtyard space in the traditional Korean house, is a good example. It has no specified purposes, but is filled with emptiness. This Madang is open and enclosed not only by structures but also by consciousness, where the community could be formed.

Walls of Silence   To exaggerate the walls is to deform the space defined by them. This can be dangerous, for they might lead to a false life. Walls do not have meaning in themselves. In the fragmented streets that mask mean and vulgar commercialism and hide the ridiculous overnight millionaire, silence is the true virtue and meaning. Walls of silence. Although the walls are made of ordinary materials, at the very least, they embrace the question of essence. The walls built by the architect with pure soul will never lose their core, will never crumble easily.

Hakdong su-jol-dang
Seoul. 1992.

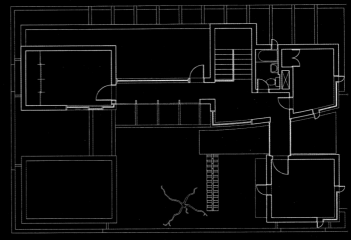

Second storey plan

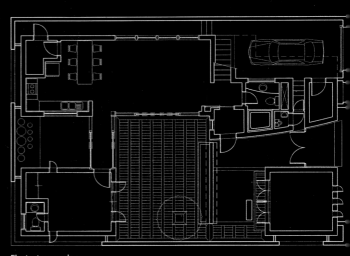

First storey plan

The madang in the 'Hakdong su-jol-dang' residence, 1992.

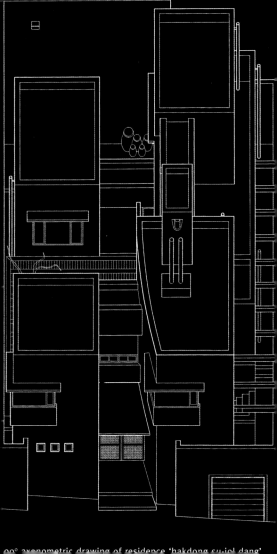

90° axonometric drawing of residence 'bakdong su-jol-dang'

'Hakdong su-jol-dang' residence, 1992.

Dolmaru Catholic Church
Tangin. 1995.

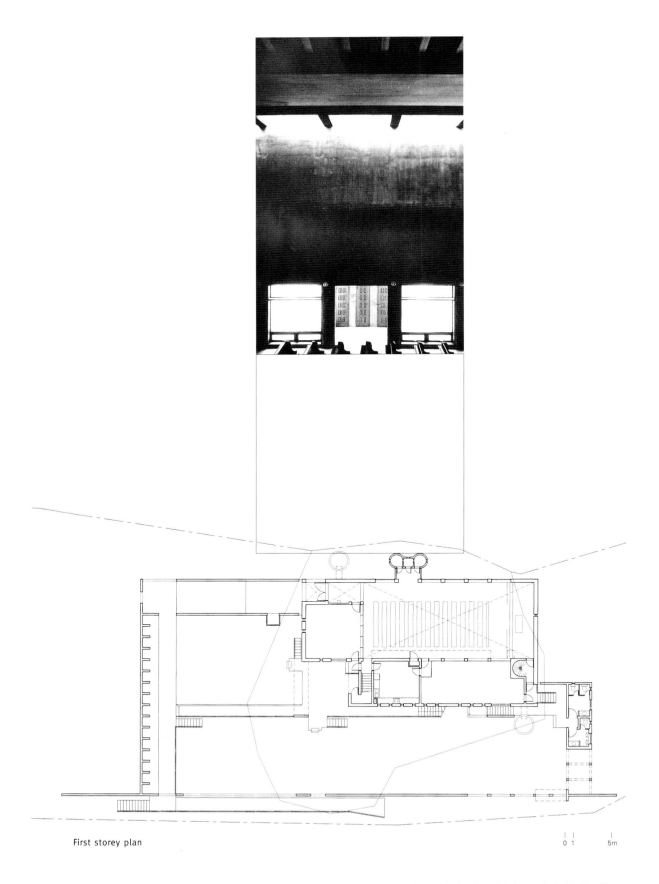

First storey plan

0 1   5m

Opposite: Interior of Dolmaru Catholic Church, 1995.

As we move into the next century, we are witnessing a predominantly 'Urban India' and an 'Urban Asia' – Bombay, Hyderabad, Kuala Lumpur, Bangkok, Shanghai, etc. are emerging into what are expected to become some of the largest urban conglomerations in the world!

Architects and designers working in these contexts are now dealing with an entire gamut of social, cultural and economic issues and problems that are often alien to these professions – where within conventional praxis, the professional architect does not engage with this wider set of issues but rather chooses to operate with the specificity of a site and in the process often becomes disconnected with the context of practice. Further, the issue of unprecedented urban growth is forcing challenges to practitioners accelerating a re-definition of the role of these professionals in society.

Thus our approach to Working in Bombay has been to use the City as a Generator of Practice, thereby not only attempting to contribute in some way to this larger issue of urbanisation as designers, but more importantly as a way for us to evolve an approach and architectural vocabulary that draw their nourishment from a powerful phenomenon – the evolving urban context. In fact, the city of Bombay has served as a laboratory from which the practice has extracted lessons through our involvement with a wide range of activities in the city. These experiences have in turn been consistently woven into our design approach. Our work with urban issues in Bombay has informed our architectural design and enabled us to evolve an architectural vocabulary that connects spatial and architectural elements from the past with a contemporary approach to building in an urban context – where a majority of our commissions are located.

In addition, being in Bombay and working from the city is unlike being based in other regional centres in India where the imposition of a region specific cultural agenda on its architects may demand that they conform to demonstrate their ethnic credentials. However, working in Bombay, in many ways, thus far, is a guarantee to a degree of conceptual freedom that permits a modulation of the traditional and contemporary – in whatever permutation one thinks is appropriate. This intertwining of times, of attitudes, of the coming together and moving apart of the past and present – is what historically has created the urban kaleidoscope of Bombay, a phenomenon that does not lend itself to simplistic readings of its form, which is pluralistic in nature and does not make explicit its origins, intentions or rationale.

In fact, the urban phenomenon of Bombay was unintended and grew in spurts over time. Bombay was not an indigenous Indian city but was built by the British expressly for trade links with India and was never perhaps expected to become a large town. Like settlements that are not expected to become large towns, Bombay was not planned. Instead, it came into being with every step of its growth being impulsive and incremental – expressing in its form the idea of the city as a field of human enterprise. This had some short-comings, for the lack of a master plan or clear overall design re-sulted in a situation where the city was always ill prepared for growth. This also offered some flexibility, for every addition or intervention was an opportunity to compensate for deficiencies or to reinforce positive attributes of the existing physical structure, which allowed the city to renew its physical expression in response to contem-porary aspirations to time.

o

Rahul Mehrotra

The City as Generator of Practice

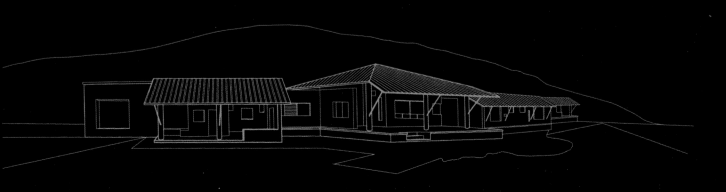

As a result, Bombay was never conceived or built in a singular image. In fact, its evolution consistently makes evident a series of dualities, a phenomenon where many worlds, many ideas and interests, influenced the city's growth. Besides an incredibly rich and varied building stock, Bombay also inherited a colonial urban diagram that survived right up to the 1950s: a dual city configuration where two worlds lived in two separate spaces. First the separation between the British and Indians and then the rich and poor. But with time, starting from the 1960s, these separate diagrams, worlds and spaces gently slipped into each other creating one space which accommodated two worlds. This was accelerated, as in most Asian Cities, by the massive shifts in demography – where waves of distress migration from the hinterlands inundated cities and irreversibly altered their very structure – both physically as well as in terms of their social makeup.

The images that emerged were those of sharp dualities – the rich and poor, images of Western cities juxtaposed with traditional icons, the city of temporary materials nestled around the city of reinforced concrete and steel. Most emblematic of the existence of these dualities in Bombay are the Bazaars in Victorian Arcades in the historic city centre where the chaotic informal sector comprising the Bazaar housed itself in the disciplined Arcades that characterise the Victorian historic core of Bombay – a situation where these extreme manifestations of urban form are physically compressed to create an incredible set of images, symbolising the emerging pluralism in the built environment of Bombay as well as in most cities in India and Asia. It was in this environment charged with duality, where 'many times' co-existed simultaneously, compressed, layered and juxtaposed with each other that lay the 'beginning' of our practice.

In this schizophrenic space and time capsule, we spent a greater part of the first three years (of our eight-year-old practice) unscrambling the patterns that made up the environment we were working in. Research became the predominant activity – the mechanism to understand the city. We looked at architecture, urban history, documented historic areas as well as contemporary urban centres and architecture, worked with conservation legislation, interacted with local history groups, worked on policies for recycling land in the city and an entire gamut of activities that engaged us with the problems of the city. Through these engagements we were exposed to the different worlds that existed in the city and the different 'times' that created these varied worlds. To cut across these differences while respecting their integrity and aspirations became somewhat an obsession. How do we as architects work for the many worlds in the city – do we respond simultaneously to the time past, present and future. How do we do this when all these times exist simultaneously? Can we design with a divided mind?

It was in this haze of experimentation that we came to re-discover the logic of Modernism, which had gallantly addressed an entire gamut of issues relevant to our society. 'Modernism' stood out – resilient and robust, withstanding the test of time. Over the years, through practice, we were further committed to the relevance of the Modernist ethos which has had a great impact on contemporary India and Asia, both in terms of its rigour and in its ability to cut across cultural differences as well as the omnipresent past that characterises most regions in Asia. This is distinct from the facile image-grabbing approach of the post-moderns or the over simplification of Modernism into a bag of aesthetic tricks in the world of advanced capitalism. Modernism in Asia, India through China, is yet linked intrinsically to its social agenda, economic rationale and political ideology: the very reasons for which these embraced Modernism when they made the transition from colonial domination. In fact, the architectural identity of post-colonial India for example, is one entirely founded on Modernism.

Thus, besides these historic antecedents, for our practice the relevance of this ethos also lies in its resilience as well as its capacity to adjust, adapt and absorb the architectural milieu of the locale. This we feel is important in a country like India, steeped in tradition, to view the culture afresh as one can through Modernism. However, through our research on the city, we were made conscious of the fact that Modernism perpetuated the *tabula rasa* mind-set in the preceding generation of Architects — one which believes "I have seen the future and it works!" In response to this situation, working in the context of Asia, the practice, besides its architectural commissions, is also committed to addressing not only the issues of the contemporary urban landscape but also to identifying aspects of our historic cities that have continuing relevance for our emerging post-colonial urbanism. The practice has thus engaged actively with urban conservation projects in Bombay with a view to facilitating the gentle transition of our historic cities into the emerging urban milieu.

Beyond urban conservation, the practice is involved with building conservation projects in Bombay. The emphasis that we have in this area of work is that of a 'creative conservation' where a critical dialogue is created between the old and new. Therefore our interest lies in the recycling of buildings and spaces where the revitalisation of a building through a pattern of contemporary use is seen as the generator of the conservation process. As architects we feel equipped to do this, because as designers one can see opportunities that exist in the re-organisation of a historic building. As a practice we have learnt a great deal about design from conservation — which has informed our work tremendously. We believe that the design of a good modern building and the involvement with conserving a historic building are not really different practices.

In fact, in our interior design projects, often in historic buildings, our approach has been to strip the space down to its bare architecture and confront it on those terms. Thus our concerns in handling interiors have clearly been spatial and architectural rather than decorative. In Bombay, like any large city in Asia or around the world, a greater bulk of work for young practice involves interior renovation, additions, alterations and new interventions. In Bombay too, the 'beginning' of our practice lay in the design of interior spaces. It was through these smaller projects that we evolved a vocabulary that has informed our architecture. Issues of layering space to create illusions of largeness, creating devices for greater flexibility and the experimentation with materials and textures all found their way into our building projects. In that sense, for us the architecture of the interior and that of the exterior become contiguous, as we apply the same set of values as well as approach to both kinds of commissions.

In our projects, the approach has been to abstract and interpret spatial arrangements as well as building elements to meet a contemporary sensibility as well as building vocabulary. The attempt is thus to combine materials, to juxtapose conventional craftsmanship with industrial materials and traditional spatial arrangements with contemporary space organisation. In short, to give expression to the multiple worlds, pluralism and dualities that so vividly characterise the Asian Landscape.

Offices for Catholic Relief Services:
A Street in the Attic
Bombay, 1993.

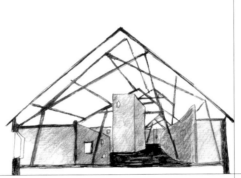

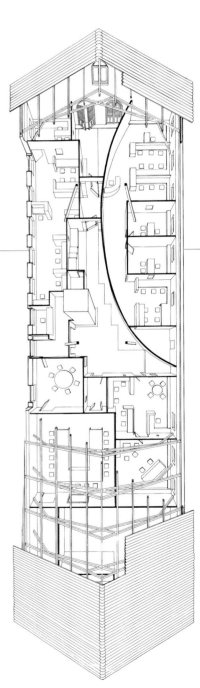

This project was commissioned by the Catholic Relief Services for a 500 sq m. office in the attic, under a spectacular timber gabled roof. The attic is in an old neo-Gothic building which has 4 storeys, each over 15 feet high, so on renting the space out to our clients, the landlord decided to construct an elevator. We created an elevator shaft running through the building and emerging in the attic, thus making the centre of the space the point of arrival. This eventually determined the entire plan of the office.

The high ceiling made air-conditioning unfeasible, so we broke up the space into small volumes, with low false ceilings. Programmatically, the space had to be broken up into a director's office,

a conference room and three administrative departments, each with a manager's office. These spaces were created using gypsum partitions and false ceilings, thereby minimising the load on the existing structure.

While doing this on a tight budget, we retained as much of the presence of the old shell as possible. The components were laid out in a manner that allowed each department their independence, yet were inter-connected with others to allow movement – all this without stepping into the non-air-conditioned attic space. The central 'walk', open to the attic roof, links these areas to the director's office and the conference rooms.

This 'street' and the

'tower block' (the lift shaft) combine to create a streetscape. More importantly, when moving within this office space, one is constantly aware of the old structure within which it sits.

Shanti – A Weekend House
Alibag. 1997.

The idea was not to have to open up the entire house if only the clients were visiting. It is configured around a courtyard that separates the two zones of the house – the main house and the two guest bedrooms. A series of parallel load-bearing walls in basalt stone were used to define the different zones. These were kept exposed on the outer surfaces and rough-plastered on the inside. The roof over the service area is a flat concrete slab while the main areas are covered with galvanised iron sheets. These appear to be lifting off the stone walls to visually accentuate their lightness. In fact, this image of light versus heavy creates a visual tension that leaves a memorable front elevation that visually responds to the profiles of the hills in the distance.

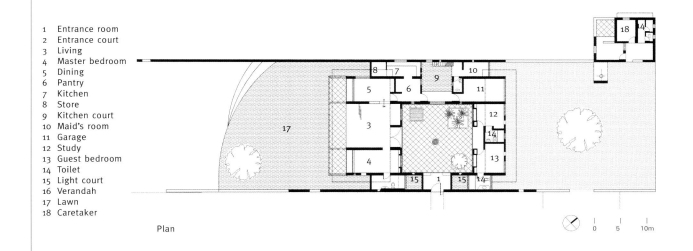

1   Entrance room
2   Entrance court
3   Living
4   Master bedroom
5   Dining
6   Pantry
7   Kitchen
8   Store
9   Kitchen court
10 Maid's room
11 Garage
12 Study
13 Guest bedroom
14 Toilet
15 Light court
16 Verandah
17 Lawn
18 Caretaker

Plan

South-east elevation   0   5   10m

Factory for S.T.P.
Goa. 1995.

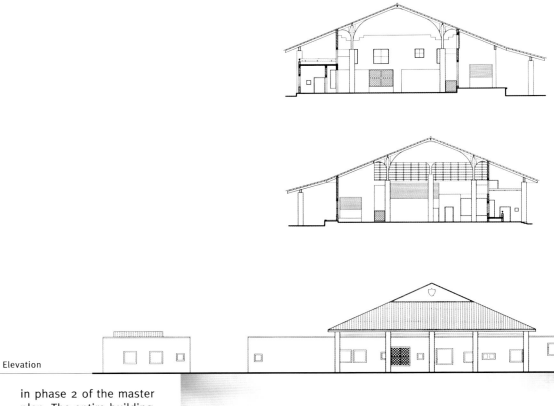

Elevation

Located in an industrial estate in Goa, this factory project required a large shed of about 1200 sq.m. as a manufacturing unit for construction additives together with ancillary functions such as research labs, administrative offices, and workers rooms. Instead of segregating these functions in separate units, we decided to wrap these architecturally more malleable functions around the factory shed, thus providing for a more integrated architectural expression.

Local laterite stone was used as a facade element which extends itself to define courtyards on either side of the building. These courtyard spaces would become the points connecting the other shed and processing units proposed in phase 2 of the master plan. The entire building is covered in a large terracotta tiled roof unifying the disparate elements housed under it.

The interior space for manufacturing is defined by circular RC columns which transform into steel brackets, articulated by bracing plates, as they make a transition to connect to the steel roof and the exposed galvanised steel sheet roofing. Skylights are placed to accentuate these structural elements. The spaces that wrap around the inner hall are more intimate in scale with ceiling tiles in terracotta which add a sense of ornament and tradition.

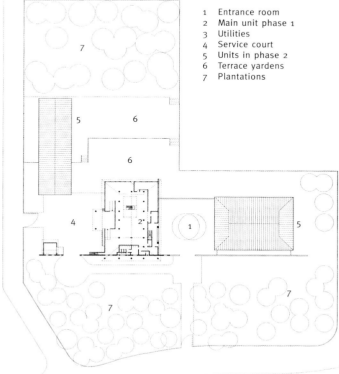

0	5	10m

1   Entrance room
2   Main unit phase 1
3   Utilities
4   Service court
5   Units in phase 2
6   Terrace yardens
7   Plantations

7

5   6

6

4   2   1   5

7   7

Site plan   0 5 10m

William Lim was born in 1932 in Hong Kong. When he recalls the society he grew up in, Lim notes the stark disparities around him, where the veneer of a thriving colonial port was juxtaposed against the poverty and decay in its underbelly. These hardships were exacerbated by the Japanese invasion and occupation during World War II. Despite his relatively privileged background and his ostensible role as an entrepreneur in private practice, much of Lim's subsequent intellectual development has been a response to the inequity he was exposed to in his youth.

These concerns were lent direction when Lim went to the progressive Architectural Association (AA) in London in 1951.[1] It was a time when Europe was undergoing intensive post-war reconstruction. The social idealism and dynamic aesthetic vision of the

"If there is one certainty in the post-modern conception of architecture it is that it is no longer about only one kind of architecture – there are many different kinds of architectures, even within one designer's or office's output, and even within one building."

Modern Movement had captured the imagination of the architectural world. AA proved an enriching experience for Lim, who was taken under the wing of John Killick, a man with a near obsession with Le Corbusier.[2] When he graduated, Lim had a thorough grounding in the tenets of Modernism in architecture.

In 1956, Lim went, on a Fulbright scholarship, to the City and Regional Planning Department of Harvard University, then under Walter Gropius. Here, his exposure to the Modern Movement grew, and he became familiar with Gropius's group working philosophy and the Bauhaus experiment. He studied planning from multi-disciplinary perspectives and developed an understanding of issues such as planning law (under Charles Haar) and land economics (taught by Lloyd Rodwin).[3] Thus began Lim's interest in urban planning and development issues. It was also the start of his long involvement and collaboration with specialists from other fields.[4]

Lim was inspired by what he learnt of Modernist architecture and planning, and was eager to put his newly acquired theories into practice to address pressing issues back home. He returned to Singapore in 1957.[5] The end of the colonial era was imminent, and Nationalist spirits were running high.[6]

Local architects wanted to strike it out on their own in the Singapore architecture scene which was then dominated by established British firms staffed by expatriates. In 1960, Lim teamed up with two contemporaries, Chen Voon-Fee and Lim Chong-Keat, to form a pioneering local firm, the Malayan Architects Co-Partnership.

1 Lim received his early education in Hong Kong. This provided him with a grounding in Chinese culture. In 1946, he returned to Singapore where he switched to an English school, which had its own Anglo-centric focus. These experiences made him comfortable with two competing cultural orientations. Growing up in Hong Kong and Singapore, the multiplicity and contradictions of colonial society were a normal part of his life.

2 Through Killick, Lim was introduced to Modernists such as Bill Howell, James Stirling and the Smithsons. He was also immersed in all things Corbusier – he visited Corbusier's built works in France, read his books extensively and attended the CIAM conference in Marseilles.

3 He also became acquainted with Jacqueline Tyrwhitt, a remarkable Englishwoman teaching at Harvard, who supported his activities and helped to put him in contact with other people of interest to his studies. Through Tyrwhitt, Lim later became involved in the World Society for Ekistics. She also actively encouraged his formation of the civil group SPUR.

4 Lim's Harvard days were also significant as it was then that he became interested in Existentialist philosophy and delved into the works of Jean-Paul Sartre and Albert Camus. These helped him to work through the relationship between 'self' and 'externality'. Particularly important were the ideas of freedom from dogma and the responsibility of the individual. These Existentialist ideas raised in Lim, quite early on, questions about Modernism itself.

5 Although Lim was born and largely educated in Hong Kong, his family was based in Singapore for many generations, and he spent different periods of his youth in each city.

6 His initial instinct to join the public sector was, however, unfeasible for various bureaucratic reasons. He then worked for three years for James Ferrie, a young and enlightened British architect.

William S. W. Lim

Pioneer, *Provocateur* and Pluralist

The most important work by the firm was the NTUC Conference Hall (1965).[7] Built in the year of Singapore's independence for use by the trade unions, the hall is emblematic of the social democrat orientation of the new nation. Architecturally, the building is a strong manifestation of the Modern Movement, with its powerfully articulated abstract forms.[8] Modernist design was thus used to express the Nationalist and Socialist ideals of the time. The building is considered a landmark in the region's architectural history.[9]

"The political and ideological images of democratic socialism must form the basis for interpretation in our physical development programme."[10]

By 1967, various problems led to the dissolution of the firm.[11] Lim then founded Design Partnership with two talented associate partners, Tay Kheng-Soon and Koh Seow-Chuan. They were determined to develop a particular working methodology for themselves.[12] The firm went on to design some of the most significant buildings of the early nation-building phase in Singapore history. These works still bore the influence of Corbusier, as well as other Modern designers and theorists. Lim describes this as the 'Heroic Period', when much creative work was produced with limited resources.[13]

Two seminal buildings are definitive of this period. People's Park Complex (1973) is composed of a high-rise residential slab block perched on a multi-functional podium.

7   NTUC is the acronym for National Trades Union Congress, the association of trade unions in Singapore. The building is also known as Singapore Conference Hall and Trades Union House. The firm won the competition to design this building in 1962.
8   Rudolph's works influenced the clear expression of service cores while Corbusier inspired the umbrella roof, which was modified to suite local climatic conditions.
9   For a more in-depth analysis of the building's significance, refer to Tan, Kok-Meng, "Critical weave: Inter-Woven Identities in The Singapore Conference Hall/Trades Union House of 1965," 1999. Unpublished article.
10 From Lim's 1967 paper "Democratic Socialism and Environmental Planning" in Lim, William, *Equity and Urban Environment in the Third World*, Singapore: DP Consultant Service, Singapore, 1975, p. 15.
11 A major source of difficulty was the division of the firm into a Singapore and a Kuala Lumpur office. Management became difficult under these circumstances and was a source of conflict. In addition, there were problems of personality incompatibilities among the partners.
12 One of the features of this office practice, in keeping with the social ideals of the partners, was the implementation of a profit sharing scheme for partners and staff members alike.

NTUC Conference Hall (1965)

People's Park Complex (1973)

The design features two inter-locking massive 'city rooms' where the teeming street activities so characteristic of Asia were brought indoors for the first time. This innovative idea was influenced by 'Metabolist' theories from Japan.[14]

Golden Mile Complex[15] (1974) is noted for being the first building in Singapore to use a stepped terrace morphology. The building also suggests a stronger connectivity with neighbouring structures, and this was an ambitious experiment to investigate new urban possibilities. It remains a stunning and original vision even today.

These two works are remarkable for their sheer scale, complexity and density as well as the ideas they embodied about modern urban life in Asia. These ground breaking projects were the first urban shopping centres and first multi-use complexes in the region and became extremely influential models[16] in the evolution and spread of this building typology in Asia for the next 20 years.[17]

In addition to advancing a Modernist direction in architectural design, Lim also pursued his interests in urban development and social justice through other forums. In Singapore, the newly elected People's Action Party (PAP) government pursued modernisation with a missionary zeal. Kampongs[18] and slums were razed and factories, public flats and roads were built at a tremendous pace.

This rapid urbanisation and industrialisation were seen by some intellectuals in Singapore to also have detrimental consequences that needed to be addressed. Lim, to-

13 For a brief history of his professional career, refer to Lim's 1997 paper "From Corb to pluralism – reflections of a Singapore architect" in Lim, William S.W., *Asian New Urbanism*, Select Books, Singapore, 1998, pp. 176–178.
14 A prominent Metabolist theorist was Fumihiko Maki, who, upon visiting the construction site of the complex, was heard to remark "we theorised it and you people are getting it built!"
15 Golden Mile Complex was originally called Woh Hup Complex.
16 Indeed, these commissions helped launch a small spate of shopping centre projects for the firm, including Tanglin Shopping Centre (1971) and Katong Shopping Centre (1973). The firm also designed Ampang Park (1973). Malaysia's first major shopping centre.
17 Refer to Bay, J.H.P. et.al. (eds.) *Contemporary Singapore Architecture.* (Singapore Institute of Architects, Singapore, 1998, p. 43.
18 *Kampongs* are vernacular village settlements comprising small clusters of timber huts.
19 The group produced two publications: *SPUR 65-67* and *SPUR 68-71.* Refer to Koolhaas's 1995 essay "Singapore Songlines: Portrait of a Potemkin Metropolis... or Thirty Years of Tabula Rasa" in Koolhaas, Rem and Bruce Mau, S, M, L, XL, 010 Publishers, Rotterdam, 1995, pp. 1008-1089. Also, refer to Naidu, Dinesh, *The Singapore Planning and Urban Research Group: SPUR and the Politics of Planning in Singapore 1965-1975*, National University of Singapore, Unpublished thesis, 1999.

gether with Tay and other architects, formed the Singapore Planning and Urban Research Group (SPUR) in 1965.[19] The group was arguably the most dynamic and critical yet rational and responsible non-governmental group in Singapore's history.[20] The work of the group, however, drew mixed responses from the authorities, and it was eventually closed down.

Another important organisation that Lim participated in was the Southeast Asian study group.[21] This was the region's first non-governmental grouping of young intellectuals specialising in different fields to investigate and discuss the problems facing the region.[22] It was a rare attempt on the part of private citizens from developing countries to collaborate to produce this level of civil initiative and depth of scholarly research.

In addition to his involvement in these two groups, Lim participated in numerous other organisations and activities such as APAC[23] and various publications.[24] He also began the practice of compiling some of his papers for publication as books, beginning with *Equity and Urban Environment in the Third World* in 1975.

"to the millions in the third world who have yet to obtain their fair share of benefits from economic development and rapid social changes"[25]

20 SPUR produced critiques and alternatives that were considered radical, including proposals for a Mass Rapid Transit system, conservation of old shophouse districts and the relocation of the civilian airport to Changi.
21 Several papers by members were compiled into the 1977 book *Questioning Development in Southeast Asia*, Select Books, Singapore, 1977.
22 Studies were made into the urban environment and mental health, the status of women and alienation and aggression in youth, amongst others.
23 Asian Planning and Architectural Collaboration (APAC) grouped emerging Asian architects: Sumet Jumsai (Thailand), Charles Correa (India), Tao Ho (Hong Kong) and Fumihiko Maki and Koichi Nagashima (Japan). They discussed the issues facing architecture in Asia. They also produced the 1980 issue of *Process: Architecture* (No. 20) titled *Contemporary Asian Architecture: Works of APAC Members*. Again, this activity was one of the few of its kind at a time when architectural discourse was largely produced by, for and about the West.
24 Lim was a member of World Society for Ekistics and to whose publication *Ekistics* he contributed articles. He was on the editorial boards of *Habitat International* (London), an international, multi-disciplinary publication, and *Solidarity: current affairs, ideas and the arts* (Manila). He sat on the board of advisors to *Mimar, architecture in development* (Paris).

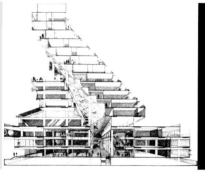

Golden Mile Complex (1974)

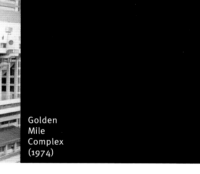

It is interesting to trace the gradual evolution in Lim's approach to urban problems over the course of the four books.[26] *Equity and Urban Environment* applies rational analysis and uses references to much statistical data to propose solutions to various problems. Many, but not all, of the articles focus on particular problems. These are classified according to topics such as 'Transportation' or 'Housing and Urban Development'. Lim argues passionately for the changes he believes need to be made to how we understand and shape our cities.

Moving to his latest book, *Asian New Urbanism* (1998), we can observe a change in his approach. The essays are, in themselves, broader and much more multi-disciplinary. They defy any neat categorisation according to topic. While still employing rational analysis, Lim stresses the importance of 'fuzzy logic' and irrationality in making sense of and solving urban problems.[27]

While some observers have noted his prophetic visions and the tendency of his proposals to get adopted by the authorities,[28] others have observed problems in his diagnosis of urban conditions.[29] Lim is not oblivious to these debates, and tries to modify and improve his propositions in the light of new evidence and arguments.[30]

The changes in the books reflect his disillusionment with Modernism as the solution to problems of urban inequity. While seeds of such doubts lay dormant in the Existentialist philosophy he was attracted to, they only came to the fore in the mid-1970s. This intellectually turbulent period also coincided with problems with the economy as well as with his professional practice.[31]

25 From the dedication in *Equity and Urban Environment*.
26 The other three titles are *An Alternative Urban Strategy* (1980), *Cities for People: Reflections of a Southeast Asian Architect* (1990) and *Asian New Urbanism: and other papers* (1998).
27 For a more detailed analysis of *Asian New Urbanism* and the changes it reflects in Lim's intellectual journey, refer to Leong, Teng-Wui and Andrew Lee Siew-Ming, " 'Asian New Urbanism' and the project of William Lim" in *Singapore Architect* (202), 1999, p. 60-63.
28 Philip Motha, in a review of *Equity and Urban Environment*, remarks "The book is replete with instances of legislative measures and official acts which were originally proposed by Mr Lim... of the other prognostications, the order in which they will come into fruition could well become a parlour guessing game."
29 Lim is often his own critic. He states in his Preface to *Asian New Urbanism*, "I predicted an impending crisis for primate cities in the Third World... This has not happened." He also notes "Another of my earlier assumptions which has gone wrong concerns the subject of energy." *Op. cit.* p. 1.
30 Lim's intellectual approach is exploratory and experimental. He operates best when he makes bold brush strokes. Prof. Kwok Kian-Woon, writing the Foreword to *Asian New Urbanism*, notes wryly that while Lim's friends in academia would like to "force him to obey our conventions", they know that "such a campaign is doomed to failure because it runs against the grain of his inimitable style."

"This [debased Modernist] approach to design ignores the environmental context, is disinterested in climatic response, and has no cultural references. In my view, the International Style of architecture has turned Modernism on its head."[32]

At this point, Lim began to question the status quo of architectural Modernism, as exemplified by the Modern Movement and its offshoot, the infamous Inter-national Style. By then, Corbusier's modular laws and other rules such as the 'Five Points of Architecture' had become either a crutch or a shackle to many architects.

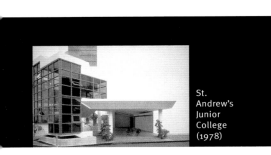

St. Andrew's Junior College (1978)

Thai House (1979)

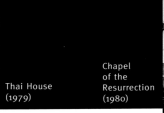

Chapel of the Resurrection (1980)

It seemed absurd to him that a great variety of building programmes were being expressed in such a controlled range of building forms. Ordinary people too were becoming weary of the proliferation of concrete boxes all around them which were supposed to be their homes, churches, schools and factories. Architecture appeared to be repetitive and unimaginative to the point of alienating people.

These problems induced in Lim a greater appreciation for diversity in architectural expression. Different building briefs called for different architectural expression. There was no need for all the building output of an era to look the same, there was no essential Zeitgeist or 'Spirit of the Age' to express in a particular way.

While moving away from Modernism, Lim sought to avoid the tendency to produce a new manifesto in the grand tradition of the avant-garde. He did not view the variety of design approaches in existence as symptomatic of aimlessness or confusion. Diversity and experimentation were seen as hallmarks of the contemporary condition itself. This attitude acted to liberate Lim from pointless stylistic battles and brought into focus, instead, the particular problems of designing individual buildings.

"Pluralism and rebelliousness are essential ingredients of good design."[33]

Post-Modernism in architecture had emerged to challenge the Modernist approach and Lim investigated this new thinking with much interest.[34] He pursued more experimental projects under the reconstituted DP Architects in the late 70s.

One work from this period that is indicative of his new direction is the St. Andrew's Junior College (1978). Institutional monotony is avoided through an informal layout and the use of bright colours to lend a convivial atmosphere to the campus. At the same time, the building retains a Modernist formal expression and a form-follows-function approach to design. The experiments he began in this project were pushed further in the design for the Chapel of the Resurrection (1980), built adjacent to the college. Lim manipulates the building form and mass with greater dexterity to break out of the Modernist mould.[35]

Lim's Post-Modern experiments during this period were not understood by his part-ners. In addition, the new directions taken by him did not secure the large and lucra-tive projects which the firm sought. These problems reached a climax in May 1981 when, within a matter of days, he made the painful decision to leave the practice.

31 By 1973, the oil crisis ended the local building boom. Another development was the exit of Tay from the firm in 1975, after which the firm was renamed DP Architects. Tay's departure resulted in more peaceful but less frequent and provocative design sessions.
32 From Lim's unpublished paper, "Journey of an Asian Architect" delivered at Tianjin University in June 1999.
33 From Lim's 1991 paper "Design Revolution" in Lim, William S.W. *Asian New Urbanism*, Select Books, Singapore, 1998, p. 79.
34 While not a disciple of any particular Post-Modernist designer or theorist, Lim has studied a range of works from the New York Five to the writings of Charles Jencks to the philosophy of Deconstructionism.
35 A smaller but similarly significant project Lim worked on during this period was the Thai House (1979). The house is noteworthy because of the freedom with which it uses curves, free form shapes, whimsical elements and diagonals in the formal design.

Unit 8 plan

Unit 8 (1984)

Tampines North Community Club (1989)

Central Square (1990)

At age 49, Lim bounced back with his own firm, William Lim Associates. He is now more confident than ever of his pluralist design approach. The practice is not locked into any one design ideology, and tries various solutions in different projects.

Another important aspect of his methodology is the stress on teamwork in the design process. He also makes it a point to acknowledge the contribution made by the whole team, as part of his committment to collaborative design. The firm recruits talented younger persons and different members of the design team are given real opportunities to contribute ideas. One of the early recruits was Mok Wei-Wei, a gifted architect who became a full partner in 1994.[36] He has collaborated actively with Lim to explore new frontiers in architectural ideas.

Lim's Post-Modern design aesthetic is given new expression in the Unit 8 (1984) luxury flats development.[37] The flat facade fronting the main road building is clad in startling pink tiles and crowned with a semicircular form. The rear of the building is an elegant series of fluid lines (balcony edges) which overlook a private pool and green valley. The sensuous balcony surfaces are punctuated by rectilinear protrusions rendered in contrasting white. His sophisticated manipulation of form, colour and space creates an exciting vision of urban domesticity.[38]

Lim makes it a point to move beyond 'pure design' to frame his work in a wider theoretical context. In addition to his involvement in various educational institutions and publications, he is a founder member and president of AA Asia. Since 1990, the group has promoted contemporary architectural discourse in Asia through seminars, study tours and other programmes.

Lim's tussles with Modernism and Post Modernism continued even as he explored other design themes and urban concerns. One of these was the issue of heritage. In his earlier works, Lim reconciled his Western training with the local context through slight adjustments to Modernist buildings in order to 'acclimatise' the design to the tropics.[39] Later designs tried to produce a vision of a specifically *Asian* modernity,[40] but this still did not deal directly with the issue of tradition.

By the 1980s, Lim began to deal with this issue more substantively in his built works. 102 Emerald Hill Road (1984) is one of many traditional terrace houses at Emerald Hill that his firm worked on. He was one of a few pioneers in Singapore in the conservation and adaptive re-use of old buildings. While the exterior facade is faithfully restored, the interior is transformed.

36 Mok, a former student of Lim at the local university, joined the firm in 1982 and became a partner in 1988.
37 See Powell, Robert (1989) *Innovative Architecture of Singapore*. Select Books, Singapore, 1989, pp. 84-87.
38 This theme in his design is developed further in the Tampines North Community Club (1989). Its pioneering use of an exuberant architectural language made it a model for a whole series of 'new generation' community centres and other buildings in Singapore. See Powell (1989) *Op. cit.* pp. 36-39. Another similar work was Central Square (1990) in Kuala Lumpur, designed in association with Chen Voon-Fee.
39 This is seen in such works as the Singapore Telephone Board Exchange (1969).
40 Examples include the Peoples Park Complex and the Golden Mile Complex.

41 From the 1987 article "Interview with William Lim – A Personal Journey and Philosophy" in Nouveau: an architectural awakening, The Architecture Society, National University of Singapore, Singapore, p. 41.

42 Since its founding in 1987, the society has embarked on conferences, talks, publications and submissions to lobby government over issues of heritage and conservation in Singapore.

43 This is a re-interpretation of the vernacular urban terrace house typology. Features such as internal courtyards, pitched roofs and a domestic scale were retained, while creativity was demonstrated in massing, spatial layout and detailing. See Powell (1989) Op. cit. pp.

44 Refer to Powell, Robert, The Asian House: Contemporary Houses of Southeast Asia, Select Books, Singapore, 1993. pp. 96-103.

45 Lim has also developed this theme in later works, including the Boon House (1992) and the Houses at Chatsworth Park (1996). See Powell, Robert, The Tropical Asian House, Select Books, Singapore, 1996, pp. 120-125. Also refer to Lim, William S.W. and Tan Hock-Beng, Contemporary Vernacular: Evoking Traditions in Asian Architecture, Select Books, Singapore, 1998, pp. 162-165.

46 Refer to Lim & Tan (1997) Op. cit.

47 He also helped organise, through AA Asia, an associated conference in September 1997 on Contemporary Vernacular: Modernising Architectural Traditions at Tsinghua Univeristy in Beijing. Refer to Chew, Christopher C.W. (ed) Contemporary Vernacular: Conceptions and Perceptions, AA Asia, Singapore, 1998.

48 Refer to Frampton's essay "Towards a Critical Regionalism: Six Points for an Architecture of Resistance" in Foster, Hal (ed.), The Anti-Aesthetic, Port Bay Press, Port Townsend, 1983, p. 17.

"I believe you do not have to abandon an architectural design approach in order to adopt another."[41]

These new directions in his practice were also mirrored in his other activities and discourse, particularly through the Singapore Heritage Society, of which Lim was a founder member and the first president.[42] While his involvement in conservation projects and heritage issues is one method of engagement with the past, he is perhaps better known for original and contemporary reinterpretations of traditional building typologies. An early exploration of this area was the Villa Chancery Condominium (1986).[43]

Certainly the most influential manifestation of this contemporary approach to vernacular forms was Reuter House (1990).[44] Here, the design was based on the colonial bungalow typology. While the house appears at first to resemble the appearance, spatial character and ambiance of the colonial bungalow, innovative differences are soon apparent in the programming of spaces, skewed planning grids and detailing. The house responds well to its two level sloping site and has tropical design features to make air-conditioning unnecessary.[45]

Lim has also been involved in the discourse over architectural regionalism through various publications, speeches and conferences. In particular, he co-authored, with Tan Hock Beng, the book *Contemporary Vernacular,*[46] which seeks to frame important Asian architectural responses to the regionalism debate.[47] Indeed, the design experiments and ideas that Lim has contributed constitute, in a sense, a response to Kenneth Frampton's call for the development of a Critical Regionalism in architecture.[48]

Clearly, Lim has explored a variety of intellectual trajectories and design possibilities over the last four decades. This diversity is a result of his plural approach to many issues. In architectural design, this has now produced another more complex and interesting manifestation. Until recently, his pluralism was seen by surveying the diversity across his various works. Yet, individual buildings often maintained cohesive identities in themselves.

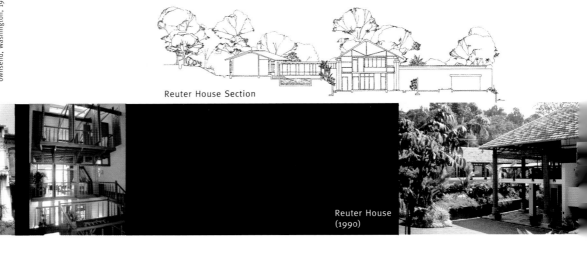

Reuter House Section

House at Emerald Hill Road (1984)

Reuter House (1990)

Now, however, Lim has begun to incorporate, within a single project, a multiplicity of design languages and elements in response to various programmatic and other demands and requirements placed on the building.

An early step in this direction is the LASALLE-SIA College of the Arts (Phase 1) (1995).[49] Lim and his team devised the strategy of redeveloping the old campus over a long time span, as funds become available. This will result in a greater complexity and diversity of design expressions. He essentially utilised a Modernist design language for Phase 1 of the project with a bold sweeping curved block. At the same time, certain spaces were rendered in different expressive forms, to suit differing requirements and to provide spatial cues for less formal interactions, as in the case of the canteen and staircases. Elsewhere, timber louvres reminiscent of vernacular buildings are apparent in corridor sunscreens.[50]

"If there is one certainty in the Post-Modern conception of architecture it is that it is no longer about only one kind of architecture – there are many different kinds of architectures, even within one designer's or office's output, and even within one building."[51]

The expression of this pluralist design philosophy within single projects is seen most clearly in two of the most recent works by William Lim Associates. The first is the Gallery Hotel, designed in collaboration with TANGGUANBEE Architects. The other is the Marine Parade Community Club.[52]

Both projects, which were completed at the turn of the millennium, signal a new stage in Lim's continuing evolution. As pioneer, provocateur and pluralist, he continues to try and expand the possibilites and scope of innovative design, theory and action in Asia.

– Dinesh Naidu

49 Refer to Look, Boon-Gee, "Stretching The Canvas: The LA SALLE-SIA College of the Arts" in *Singapore Architect* (190), 1996.
50 Even as these design experiments continue, the firm continues to use other approaches and languages, as in the case of the Cahaya House project in Malaysia.
51 Borden, Iain, "Revolution" in *Blueprint* July/August 1999, pp. 37 -38.
52 See Van Schaik, Leon, "Social Condensers: The Club as a Social Force" in the catalogue *Community Clubs 1986-1999: William Lim Associates* for an exhibition was held at RMIT that compares two community clubs by the firm: Tampines North and Marine Parade.

LASALLE-SIA College of the Arts, Phase 1 (1995)

Cahaya House (1995)

The Gallery Evason Hotel

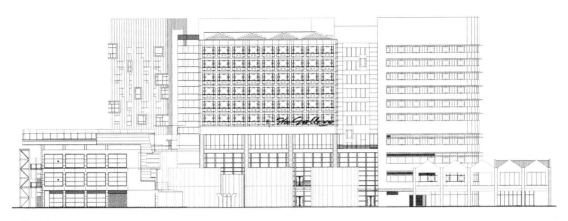

Elevation

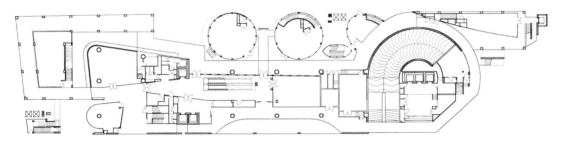

First storey plan

Assembling the Marine Parade Community Club (MPCC) 2000
– Leong Teng Wui and Andrew Lee

How did you approach the design of the MPCC project?

Finding the initial design strategy for the project took quite a while. The struggle lay in establishing the defining parameter for the project – in establishing what were the important architectural opportunities unique to the project. Sometimes a design strategy can be quickly established by fixing a particular direction of experimentation at the onset. In the case of the MPCC project, the intention was to defer the fixing of any preferred design meanings. The design direction was more ambiguous. We tried not to be too conscious of infusing the project with a particular meaning too soon. The ability to let the imagination unfolds without too much preconceived hang-ups about what the end product might be resulted in the generation of interesting but at times opposing ideas. These ideas arose at times out of opportunities, at other times out of necessity. The length of time taken to define the design parameter had to do with the testing and selection of these ideas. We had to weigh what was important and what could realistically be achieved.

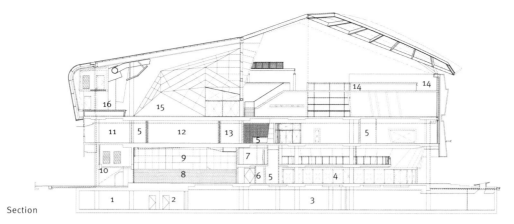

Section

1 A/C room
2 CD shelter
3 NLB offices
4 Office
5 Circulation
6 WC
7 Changing room
8 Theatrette
9 A/V control room
10 Carpark lot
11 Homecraft room
12 Karaoke room
13 Multi-purpose room
14 Gallery
15 Multi-purpose sports hall
16 Stage

2 The site of the MPCC project was characterized by its strategic corner location as well as the predominantly HDB landscape. Did the design attempt to deal with any of these considerations?

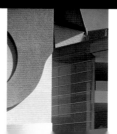

The obvious challenge was how do you begin to address the corner location. Do you attempt to mark the corner location by the placement of spatial objects? Do you attempt to infuse its corner location with a strong iconic presence? The client's preference was for the placement of an identifiable clock tower at the road junction. The conceptual image of the design team however was based on the idea of an assemblage of differentiated building "skins" acting as surfaces that would give shape to the building edge. It was an attempt to delineate the various complex and different programs within the building. The opaque skin would define the community club, the transparent skin would define the library while the metallic roof skin would define the auditorium – the whole of the building being the overlapping and maneuvering of its various parts.

The absence of any site boundary wall was an intentional decision to remove any possible obstructions of the circulation flow from the surrounding buildings to the MPCC. The design intent was to occupy the "void deck" of the MPCC as a usable stratum, being filled with a section of both the community club and the library and a café as well. It offers the possibility of slowing down the sequence of movement from the HDB blocks, allowing for a more active engagement with the "void deck" of the MPCC. Perhaps if we have a chance to design another similar project within an HDB area, we will consider the option of lifting up the whole building on columns, as a public building that can also be an appropriate response. However given the proximity of the surrounding HDB blocks within the current site, more units of flats would have had their views obstructed if the building had been further lifted.

3 Your firm had previously designed the Tampines North Community Centre. What is your attitude towards the use of past models in the design process?

4 The open space under the series of floating curve metal roofs in the MPCC project is extremely evocative – evocative in the sense that it defies the conventional perception of an architectural space. One does not know where the enclosing wall starts or ends or whether the space is considered outside or inside. Its intended utilitarian use is that of a multi-purpose space that could function as a shared communal space, a basketball court or a gallery. Was there a conscious attempt to represent the building as a social condenser – as an image of an assembly sharing a common place under an architectural element?

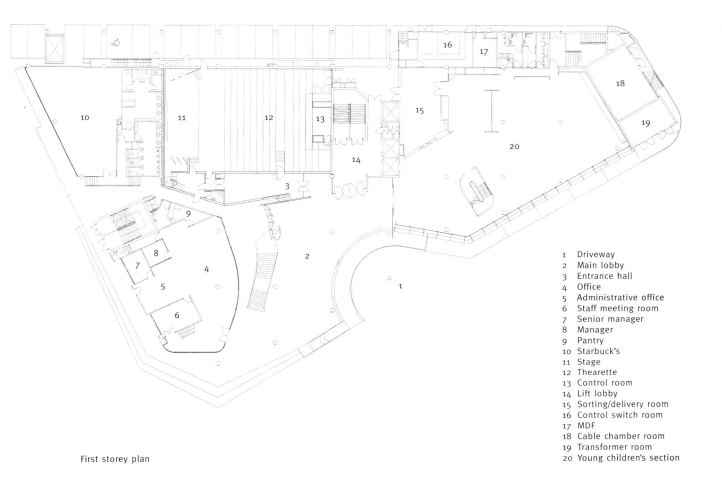

First storey plan

1 Driveway
2 Main lobby
3 Entrance hall
4 Office
5 Administrative office
6 Staff meeting room
7 Senior manager
8 Manager
9 Pantry
10 Starbuck's
11 Stage
12 Thearette
13 Control room
14 Lift lobby
15 Sorting/delivery room
16 Control switch room
17 MDF
18 Cable chamber room
19 Transformer room
20 Young children's section

We are interested in past models not in the sense of replicating what was previously built but in understanding how certain strategic decisions can affect the architectural firm's control of the design process.

The experience gained in terms of understanding the client's decision-making mechanism and the various checkpoints was useful. The client's design review committee has not changed much since the days of TNCC. Being a community development organization, the client had a set of working procedures and a working budget that had to be closely adhered to. For example, the budget for the MPCC did not include the fees for a signage or landscape consultant. The client's usual method of practice was to conduct a tender exercise to award the contract to the lowest but not necessarily the better quality contractors. We decided to design the signage and landscape concept. We considered that the result would be having better control and versatility over the design process.

We did not try to deliberately represent the building as an absorber of social meanings. The intention was not so much to "re-present" a particular type of social space as in trying to optimize and intensify the way in which spaces and events can cross-mix beneath the structural roof. This is not to suggest that the building is devoid of any social concerns. We were interested that the main users, namely the HDB heartlanders, deserved the best effort the design team could muster. Every possibility was rigorously tested throughout the design process. Goh Kasan, the project architect who was mainly responsible for the structural roof design, has designed at least one hundred working models. Of course it was not just a formalistic exercise. If it had been, most people might have stopped at four or five working models.

Asia Modernising: The Projects of William Lim Associates
– Leong Teng Wui and Andrew Lee Siew Ming

Asia Modernising – Emergent 'Scapes'

The fluid, borderless and flexible movement of global capitalism that is producing much of the emergent urban 'scapes' around the world and new modalities of modernity raises important ethical questions for architectural theory and practice. Global capitalism can be a highly homogenising force that constantly threatens the extinction of specificity, the erasure of memories and the effacement of differences in the heartland. Nowhere is this homogenising tendency more visible and visceral than in the rapid urbanisation of the Asian-Pacific region.

Architectural practice, in the service of powerful transnational clients and foot-loose mammon seeking the highest returns, can be notoriously blinkered and complicit in reproducing much of the banal anonymous urban environments and ubiquitous sense of "placelessness" around the world. Driven by the pressures of rapid urbanisation and commercial speculations, pattern-book architectural styles and forms are often appropriated in a cynical and unfiltered

5 **What is the relationship between the design of a community club and the practice of contemporary art?**

manner, regardless of their relevance and appropriateness for the city and its specific contexts. This 'occidentalist' approach has resulted in a bland ubiquity across the cities of Asia. Witness the proliferation of anonymous dumb boxes to decorated sheds with 'classical' pretensions to Disneyesque theme-parks developments. On the other hand, the 'orientalist' response to this 'internationalism' can be equally reductive and problematic. Privileging certain regional 'origins' and indigenous 'essence', there is also a regressive tendency to re-appropriate traditional forms (ranging to Balinese to Malayan) to fit modern functions. The results are invariably a form of degraded orientalist kitsch, a type of decontextualised "decorated shed", which are as equally homogenising and intellectually impoverished as the 'internationalist' camp.

Yet, the rhizomatic dynamics of global capitalism is also rich in its possibilities. The unprecedented intensity of interconnectedness between cultures, societies and people holds the promise of a new cultural and intellectual pluralism; and a cosmopolis that is 'liberated' from the nightmares of insular traditions. Thus one key challenge that confronts architecture as an ethical project is this : how to resist the homogenising force of globalisation, but yet not negating the opportunities to plumb the rich depths of an interconnected, complex global modernity for experimentation, innovation and change? Are there urban strategies which could enable and empower new social spaces which support multiplicity, diversity and complexity? Are there architectural strategies which transcend the usual dichotomies of East/West to offer an innovative response to globalisation?

Two Projects

The recently completed Marine Parade Community Club (MPCC) at Marine Parade Road and the soon to be completed Gallery Evason Hotel (GEH) at Robertson Quay in Singapore offer some interesting lessons on one possible approach in thinking and making architecture in the new Asian urbanism. Complex and yet specific, the projects offer compelling insights into the making of a new kind of hybrid space, which could be described as the indeterminate, in-between state of being simultaneously both global and local, universal and specific in its constitution. Rich in inventive possibilities for architecture, the hybrid project offers one way in which the practice of architecture could operate in a transgressive mode, within an "in-between" framework that does not reduce nor efface differences. It is this sensitivity to differences and the pluralistic mindset that acknowledge complexity which one could argue as 'ethical'.

In the past, works of art which are produced went directly to either the living room of rich patrons or the exhibition hall of art museums. Architecture often becomes the backdrop for the foregrounding of art works. In the MPCC project, we do not envisage the building as a mere container of exhibition spaces for the display of art works but much more as the test case of how contemporary art practices in Singapore can be re-shaped. A competition is held to procure the piece of public art. The competition invites artists from the Southeast Asian region to submit proposals by utilizing the curved architectural facade as the canvass for the artwork. This is the meaning of the prominent curved art wall – the grafting of an artwork onto an architectural element. This involves a transaction from which both art and architecture can benefit by gaining qualities that lie outside its own framework. This has resulted in an altered way of perceiving contemporary art practice, dislocating an artwork from say its interior position in a museum and fusing it with the exterior wall façade of the building. By virtue of its prominent location and sheer size, the art wall is already provoking strong responses from the community and the general public.

Even the creative team behind it – William Lim Associates1 for the MPCC, and in collaboration with Tang Guan Bee for the GEH - operated as a form of loose multiplicity. Thus, while it is tempting to differentiate the individual firm and personalities' contributions to the projects, it cannot be so easily reduced or attributable because the project defies such easy reduction. Both practices and their cast of characters brought with them their strengths, bias, idiosyncrasies and differences. Indeed, the conceptualisation and execution of the building would arguably be 'impoverished' without this strategic collaboration. This strategic alliance represented a transgressive, pluralistic practice which are inherently more strategic and able to exploit better the opportunities for innovation in an increasing complex urban environment.

The Hybrid Project – Co-location, Reciprocity and Materiality

Taking the MPCC as a case study (the GEH will be covered in greater details in a later issue of the Asian Architect), three strategies could be discerned which are considered characteristic of the "hybrid" condition. They are Co-location, Reciprocity and Materiality.

These strategies are not static classifications, nor are they meant to be exhaustive. By themselves, each concept posits and articulates inventive possibilities between the global and the local, the universal and the specific, East and West. Collectively they constitute an open-ended relational system with other to produce a rich matrix of new relationships that continuously dismantle and disrupt binary thinking. The strategies are loosely articulated to offer not as definitive formulae, but as thought cues and triggers for the readers to develop their own multiple readings and associations about the MPCC.

Co-location

Responding to the land-scarce condition in Singapore, the MPCC is planned as a medium-rise, high-density hybrid building which are to co-locate various community programmes in the heartland of a public housing estate. It has cross-programmed a community and recreational facilities like a roof-top basketball court, a regional library, cafes and a performing arts theatre. The MPCC also has a community-bonding function in that it act as a social 'condenser', and a social space for the various multi-racial communities to share these programmes.

6 **The design of contemporary community clubs has increasingly accommodated a multiplicity of programs, which include cafés, libraries, black-boxes, practice rooms, basketball courts, auditoriums, classrooms to name a few. How do you attempt to organize this hybrid of programs?**

Unlike conventional community clubs in Singapore, these programmes are not held together as a hierarchical, visually coherent whole. Instead, it is a loose and fragmented assemblage with overlapping public voids and interstitial situations. The rich network of public spaces and programmes suggested a complex social space – collective, pluralistic and yet able to accommodate differences. As a 'hybrid' space, it is able to 'co-locate' and accommodate the multiplicity of programmes in a non-deterministic, non-dominated state. As none of these programmes dominates but flows and intertwines with each other, the 'hybrid' condition is experienced both as a fluid unfolding landscape and as specific spatial moments though the complex assemblage of events and spaces. These spatial moments are at once 'globalised' and 'localised' as the users and uses interact in complex ways, suggesting interesting social possibilities in a non-dominating sense.

Reciprocity

The hybrid space is inherently rhizhomatic, unpredictable and multivalent. The hybridity is characterised by a non-hierarchical framework of reciprocal relations between different programmes, elements, spaces, materials and social conditions. This combination of fragmented and multiple relationships constantly break down the conventional hierarchy of systemic representations and meanings to open up new ways of living, working, thinking and seeing. New identities are thus re-defined even as they re-define the new realities.

One of the most striking feature of the MPCC is the art-mural 'skin'. The art-mural wall, commissioned as the winning result of a regional competition, is 'grafted' as part of the 'skin' that wraps around the community club and is sited at the most prominent corner that fronts Marine Parade Road. In this gesture, the MPCC challenged the conventional representation of institutional types. The corner, often a space of contestation for public symbols because of its visibility and prime frontage, is given over to an public artwork rather than the traditional icons of institutional power

Given the differing programmatic demands, it was difficult to define the building solely from a single pre-planned order of regularity and cohesiveness. On the contrary, the intention was to adopt a combination of strategies which would favour the staging of diverse possibilities among the different programs. It was not an issue of clearly defined forms but of discovering conventional hybrids.

Sometimes we opted to combine the admixture of programs into a series of non-conventional building forms. For example, the community club section is expressed as an art object that fuses with the building façade while the basketball court is expressed as a set of leaf-like metal plates colonizing the roof.

At most times, the placement of the various programs arose out of sheer necessity. The decision to connect or separate a sequence of spaces is often determined by the programmatic constraints. For instance the community club being the initial owner of the land insisted on retaining for itself the prominent corner site although the library board as co-occupant was occupying nearly 60% of the total area. The library board agreed to the arrangement but insisted on a separate architectural expression for the library.

In addition, in the library section of the building, we proposed using the internal freestanding staircase as a conveyor of history. Besides tracing the historical development of the library through a series of narratives, we inserted an architectural element – a window grille from the previous library that was pulled down recently. Here the use of "memory" as a connector of human experiences was adopted – the reading of the building being the aggregate of the various fragmentary and diverse expressions.

(like the ubiquitous clock tower). The 3-dimensional wall relief with its digital messages, neon lights, swirling motifs and 'cyclone eye', is particularly ambiguous and evocative of complex meanings and associations. It has been drawing a wide range of reactions from the members of the public, and it is this active reciprocity that suggests a more enriching social space between the building, the uses and the users.

Materiality

The hybrid space recuperates a new phenomenological interpretation of the site through the interest in the materiality of the project. The choice and combination of materials, the techniques of working and using the materials, the placement and particular constructional methods could reveal certain insights and knowledge about how the different forces shaped the project. This physicality is potentially transformative as it could re-establish new place and

7 A number of materials are used in the MPCC design. How do you choose a particular material, for example corrugated metal or glass mosaics, in the building?

experiential qualities, which might otherwise be effaced or reduced.

For instance, the juxtaposition and interlocking of the more transparent ribbon-window box of the library with the more opaque art-mural skin around the corner podium suggested a more complex representation of the 'institution'. The use of brightly coloured mosaic tiles, glass-enclosed units, the neon night lighting, and the roof gestures, the playful details convey a host of popular associations – cinema, dance hall, cabaret club, shopping centre – which may not detract from the essential social function of the MPCC as a populist but also consumer-driven space in the public housing heartland.

Less aesthetics, more ethics in a modenising Asia
As a region that is rapidly changing, how does architecture play a role in "humanising" the alienating aspects of globalisation? In the increasing privatisation of the public realm by global capitalism, can the design profession innovate new kind of non-exclusionary social spaces in the Asian city where the collective experience is still possible

8 How do you think end-users will react to the MPCC building?

We set ourselves the problem of redefining preconceived expectations of how materials can be used. For instance, it took a while to convince the client that corrugated metal sheet should be used despite its familiar associations with an industrialized image – it looks like an industrial building in Jurong. Corrugated metal is now a much more refined material and there is no reason why it cannot be adopted even in prestigious projects. We have experimented with the material in the LaSalle Art School – a project that is located within a good class bungalow precinct. We cladded the external curved façade with corrugated metal. In the MPCC project, besides using the material to define the external curved roof, the corrugation came much more strongly into play inside the building. We think that the impact on the viewer when perceiving the metal corrugation in the proposed multi-purpose hall is much more telling, because it does not represent an accepted image. It is an image that is not commonly expected.

As was the case with the metal corrugation, the clients voiced their reservations over the choice of glass mosaics, associating the material as a throwback to a dated old-fashioned past. Our decision on the other hand was made to infuse the tactile aspect of the exterior art wall within some of the internal circulation routes. As elements of movement and transition, these spaces describe the interface between architecture and the moving viewer. By employing the reflectivity of glass mosaics, these normally subdued circulation routes are re-coded into a spatially different matrix and experience. The intention is for the viewer who walks through the MPCC to constantly construct a changing image of the building.

for both cosmopolitans and heartlanders? Can the profession exploit the pluralism and multiplicity inherent in a cosmopolitan city to enrich its ability to create real and meaning places for diversity of different groups? What are the new kind of structures, forms and spaces that would be the most potent expression of the cosmopolis?

Through its complex and multi-faceted qualities, the MPCC have offered some pointers on one possible modality of critical engagement with globalisation: that the hybrid project could be modern, global and yet 'local' in its engagement with a globalising Asia. Transcending the usual cliched dichotomies and the aesthetics of object-fixation, the hybrid project is first and last an ethical enterprise. An enterprise that constantly attempts to re-locate architecture within the larger socio-historical, psychic context of the city, but without the hubris and deterministic ethos of high modernism. Ultimately, the unfinished projects of William Lim and his collaborators are themselves the mirror of this emerging "hybrid" condition – complex, pluralistic and transgressive – as the hallmark of the new Asian urbanism.

1   For this essay, when reference is made to the architect "William Lim", it is intended as a shorthand to signify the team of partners/architects/students collectively known as William Lim Associates (WLA). Willie is well known for this collaborative approach as a creative process as much as a design strategy. For instance, Willie's ex-partner, Teh Joo Heng provided much of the project management and coordination that was crucial to the successful execution of the design intentions for the Gallery Hotel. Willie has also developed a "fuzzy" design methodology that actively pursue multiplicity of approaches, inputs and plurality of expressions. Indeed, the cast of talents in WLA provided much of the diversity, energy and frisson so critical to the creative enterprise.

We expect a different and multi-layered reading, ranging from simple to complex responses. The response can be as simple as seeing the MPCC as a fun place. To some end-users it might well become a popular place to hang out and relax. The HDB heartlanders must be able to feel comfortable. One can come into the MPCC in a pair of shorts and slippers, walk into the library to borrow a book and eventually end up in the corner café for a nice cup of coffee. There is really no pretension or hang-up to depict the building in terms of some fixed historical or cultural leitmotiv in order for the end-user to appreciate the building.

On the contrary the design intention is to free the design process from a tendency towards fixed types and expectations. The design process should permit the assembling of the collective to be conceived from a fresh perspective, no longer seen as the mere organizer of functional dictates and requirements. The intention is not for architecture to be viewed as a problem-solving machine that fixes prescribed patterns of usage between the physical environment and the experiencing users. The aim is the inverse – to encourage spatial moments where the conventional relationship between the built environment and the experiencing users is constantly altered or changed. In this way, the users are allowed to appropriate and re-interpret the way in which some of the spaces can be used. It will be interesting to see how well the MPCC will work out in this aspect.

Architecture is basically a field of thoughts and the architect is a person of thought who expresses him/herself in this field. In this context, the explanation of buildings that are designed by architects passes through the explanation of their thoughts and anxiety. Identity, morality and legacy are one inside the other for the architect and his/her architecture. The performance of this system depends upon the set of rules and acceptances the architect has envisioned for him/herself. In spite of a general sense of freedom, the architect is in a regulated system of values. This has to be explanatory, coherent and "correct" with its own internal reason even if others do not accept it. For the architects who "construct", this proposition begins where the vocal statement ends. The building exists. We can come up with thousands of reasons trying to explain that it actually is not what we had thought of, but this does not change the way the building exists. It only reveals our desperation. It is perhaps because architecture can only be done by stubborn insistence.

Thoughts exist in the beginning, formed by constructing, and again return back to the initial point:

Experience is personal for the architect. It is gained by directly constructing. In spite of this, architecture is not an activity of invention but one of investigation. The past gives us clues of how our future should be. The present is formed with this knowledge. Many things which we assume are "new", come out of our accumulation. Nothing exists from non-existence nor disappears while it exists. For this reason, it is important to take place in the memory of the city. Memory comprises the entire historical process which can be known.

Every building, besides meeting the needs of the functions it is designed for, is a value itself. Therefore, it has to be considered exceptionally and independent from function too.

The nearby geography is an important factor. A building only exists for and at the place of its own. It neither can be carried to somewhere else nor can be totally understood when abstracted from its own environment.

Whatever the monetary possibilities are, to produce at an inexpensive cost is an important matter. It is an obligation for an architect to have a serviceable accumulation of knowledge about the systems, details and the materials in order to achieve this.

It is significant to belong to the entire epoch or to be untimely rather than belonging to the current period.

The building is envisioned from the exterior towards the interior as well as from the interior to the exterior. In spite of the inevitable relationship between the interior and the exterior, the exterior is not a result formed by itself. It has to be considered particularly and separately. The parameters of this consideration are totally different from the ones of the "interior". To find the common solution for both the interior and the exterior without growing distant from both of their wills makes the "wall" which stands just at the intersection of them the most fundamental architectural component.

The environment is not necessarily a value with which a harmonious relationship should be established. A relationship of incongruity too is something to speak of. The decision is closely concerned with the sort of environment we are in at that moment.

Every fragment of the building has special significance. They should be treated as the way they are and with the interrelation they have between each other together with the whole. The basic diagnosis is their relationship with the whole.

As the buildings are programmed by the requests of the users, the users might as well be programmed by the demands of the building. Architecture is, by this means, insistent. It is composed of a system of thought and comprises a system of living.

The interior analysis should be flexible enough to meet the possible modifications through time whilst the solutions of the use objectives of the building are carried on. A building is not yet finished when handing it over to its users. It continues to form during time depending upon its quality, but this formation

Nevzat Sayin

Architecture as the Construction of Thoughts

The main problem is not metamorphosis but continuity. For this reason, it is more important to have the idea of "the state of belonging" rather than doing something original. In spite of keeping a sense of the "past", it should concern itself with a unique architectural language.

Strength and permanence are basic elements of architecture. The foresight concerning the question of "No building will be able to exist as it is, so how will they survive?" determines what is needed to be done at the present.

The simplicity of construction and its capability to be treated roughly are relevant to the ways and habits of construction and the use of the building. These factors determine the selection of the materials, prediction of the details and gradually the principles of design.

The building should be clearly and easily understood by its users although it is assembled on a complex story with its interior and exterior resolution. Therefore "reduction" is a significant concept.

The easy comprehension released out of such a complex story makes up the tension within the inertness of the building. Tension, if spread out all over the building, causes uneasiness whereas with its presence at crucial spots, it creates "excitement".

No one ever tells the architect what the building they wished for would look like. At the most, they can only tell "what" they want. The overall results belong to the architect. In the end, it comes into being what we wish to transform that building into which had been a concept at the beginning. Accordingly, the architect is totally responsible for the conclusion.

Irmak High School

Istanbul. 1999.

This is a high school building among other existing buildings, trees, a main road and the sea in the middle of the city at the Asian side of Istanbul. The programme is a typical high school programme, except with a few differences. We thought of a huge "hall" as a space in which exist units for various purposes, separated by simple sections. It is a void that is illuminated, tranquil, as though it is the "outside". The view of the building from around is a closed box of simple geometric forms just to defy the chaotic structures surrounding it. The copper roof makes the sense of being sheltered more evident.

To give a sense of order, the interior spaces were place on axes which may be easily understood though not seen when looked at. The glass walls of the classrooms and the transparency of the other walls facing the inner corridors and the outer terraces make the spaces flow into each other and out to the exterior. The terraces on the southeast side help to maintain a controlled illumination of daylight. By placing the dining and the sports hall at the sea side and the conference hall at the street side, it is proposed that they could serve other activities since there are no such places at close vicinity. Both prefabrication and traditional systems of construction were used, with traditional methods being industrialised. As a result the construction site turned out to be an assembling site.

General view of the high school

View of the conference hall

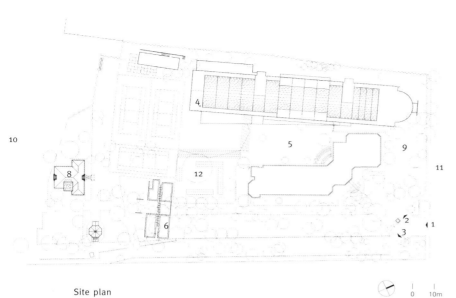

Site plan

1   Main entrance
2   Campus entrance
3   Entrance to the historical building
4   Highschool
5   Playground & protocol area
6   Kindergarten
7   Elementary school
8   Historical building
9   Parking lot
10 The Marmara Sea
11 Main street
12 Monumental tree

0   10m

Top: View from the sea, facing southwest
Left: Southeastern facade, looking to the playground.

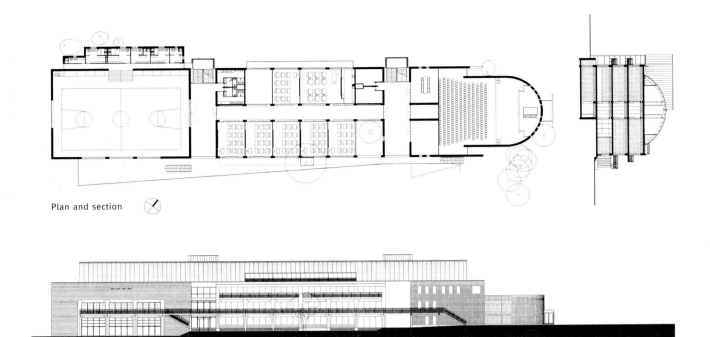

Plan and section

Southeast elevation

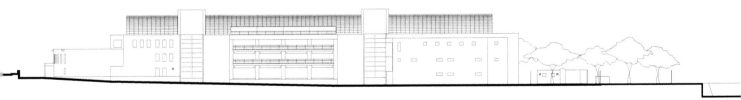

Northwest elevation

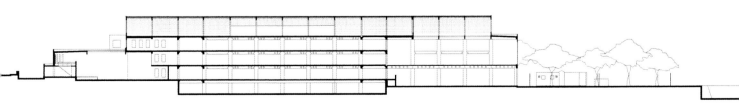

Section

0   5   10m

Bottom: The vault   Right: View from southeast

Pulver and Solvent Industrial Buildings

Istanbul. 1998.

Two totally independent factory buildings, with separate garbage rooms, productive and administrative spaces, share the same main entrance. One of them produces electrostatic powder coating materials (solvent) and the other thermoplastic elastomer (pulver). The transformation plant and the heating system located beyond the outer walls and the buildings are of exposed concrete made during the process of construction. The factory and the office spaces were prefabricated off site.

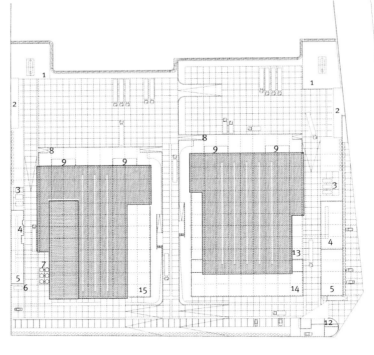
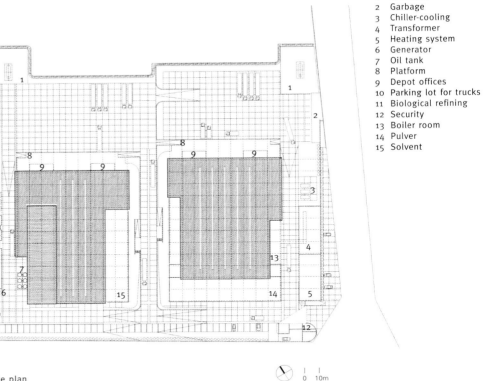

1 LPG tank
2 Garbage
3 Chiller-cooling
4 Transformer
5 Heating system
6 Generator
7 Oil tank
8 Platform
9 Depot offices
10 Parking lot for trucks
11 Biological refining
12 Security
13 Boiler room
14 Pulver
15 Solvent

Site plan

0   10m

Top left: View from the west   Top right: View from the northwest   Bottom right: The main entrance

Section

Elevation

0   10m

Top (from left to right): Boiler room of Pulver; entrance hall of Pulver; office floor of Pulver
Left: Roof structure of Solvent

Gorener House
Balikser. 1997.

In between a grove of olive trees, a new building is added to an existing one. It is of steel and wood – light and flexible in contrast with the immovable invariables of the existing situation. The inertia of the stone at the sloping land transforms into steel and wood as the slope rises – a geometric and volumetric echo of the topography. The stone is left as it is – the continuity of memory in geography.

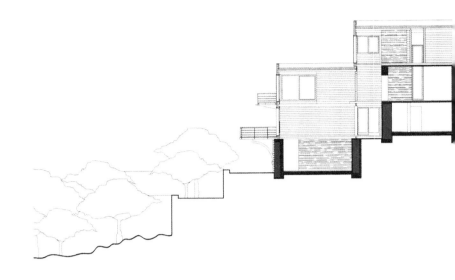

East elevation

View from southeast

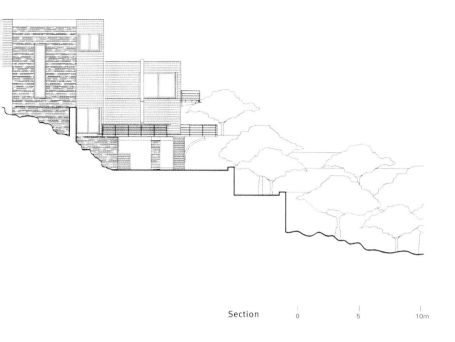

Section   0   5   10m

View from the south

South elevation

0   5   10m

Stairs from the terrace

Stairs to the basement

Third storey plan

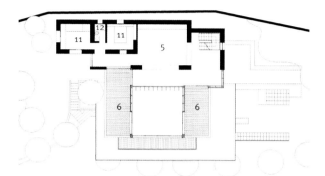

Second storey plan

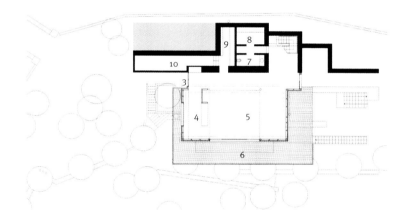

First storey plan

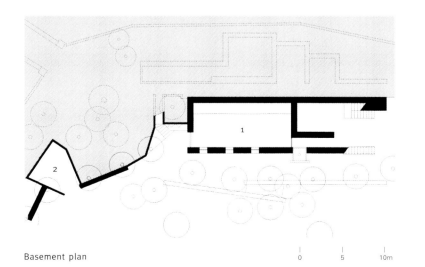

Basement plan

1	Storage
2	Heating system
3	Entrance
4	Kitchen
5	Living & dining
6	Terrace
7	WC
8	Laundry
9	Pantry
10	Storage
11	Living
12	Terrace
13	Bedroom
14	Bathroom
15	Dressing room

Staircase of the interior

0   5   10m

Gon 2:
Leather Products Manufacturing Factory
Istanbul. 1995.

A closed box when approached from outside, the building does not seem to exist when you are inside. There is nothing else to be perceived except the void containing the planes holding the machines and the people in the interior space.
It is an industrial building bearing only what is necessary inside.
Reinforced concrete is the only material used. Disregarding any coating and the plastering, the building was finished after removing the moulds and putting in the joinery elements. The building has been given the National Architectural Award by the Turkish Chamber of Architects of Istanbul in 1996 and was nominated for the Aga Khan Award for Architecture in the same year.

View from the west

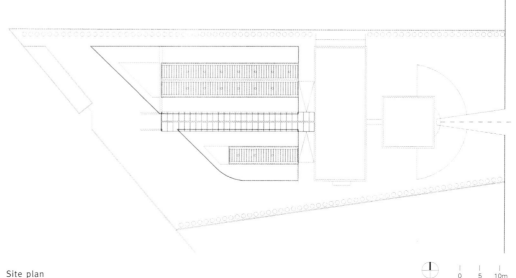

Site plan

0   5   10m

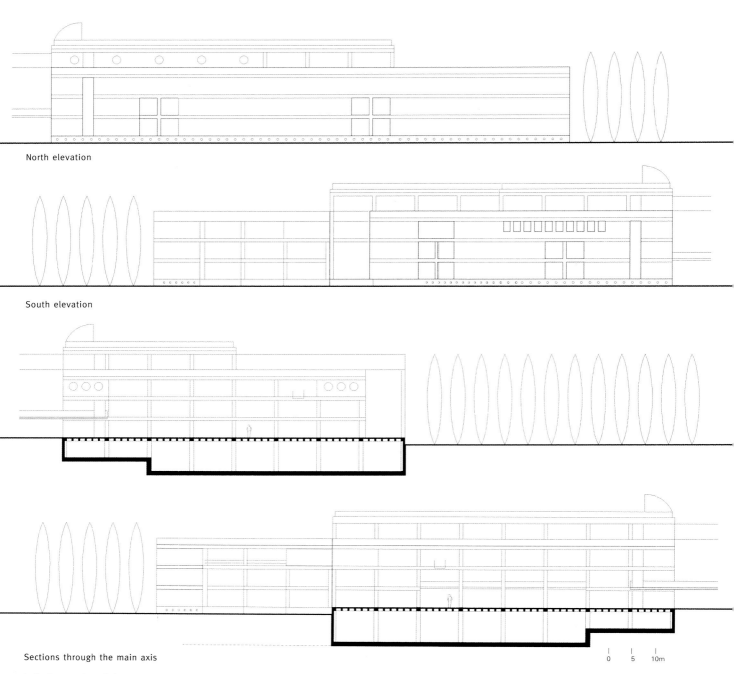

North elevation

South elevation

Sections through the main axis

0 5 10m

Left: Perspective of the main axis through the west   Right: Perspective of the main axis

"Mekik": a 'void' inside

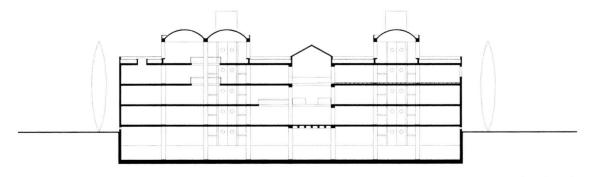

Section through the shop floor

0   5   10m

Lokman Sahin House

Tekirdag. 1997.

This is a 800 sq m. building formed by three parts and the interconnections of their open/close spaces on an empty piece of land which has been used for agricultural purposes in a forest. Standing as far as it could at the sloping landscape in a north/south orientation, a solid back wall facing north was erected to block the shrill wind. The front/south facade which faces the area of the settlement is kept open. The building has been given the National Architectural Award by the Turkish Chamber of Architects of Istanbul in 1998.

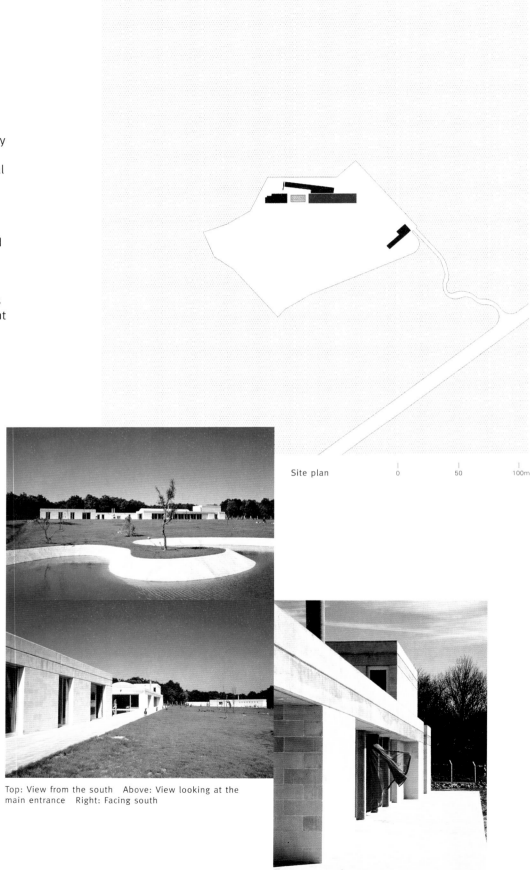

Site plan   0   50   100m

Top: View from the south   Above: View looking at the main entrance   Right: Facing south

Bottom: Detail of the facade
Right: Living room

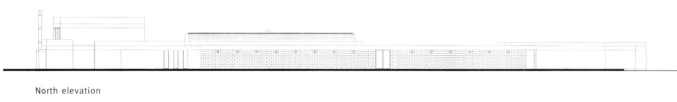

North elevation

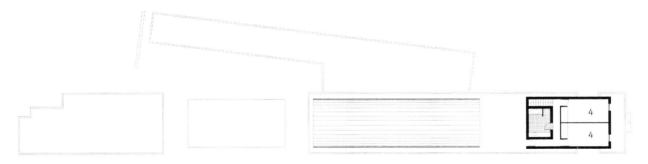

Second storey plan

1 Entrance
2 Kitchen
3 Living
4 Bedroom
5 Archive & storage
6 Fitness
7 Pool
8 Guest house
9 Parking lot

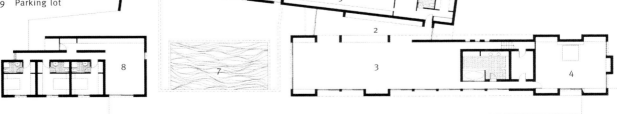

First storey plan

0   5   10m

Chang Yung-Ho ___

Dense Urbanism and Miniature Cities

Parallel City
A bookstore in Nanchang. 1996.

Most apartment blocks built in the 1950s to the early 1980s in China were long and narrow buildings that epitomise the uniformity of an architecture that is provided by the state as social welfare. Collectively, the housing projects make up a "parallel city". This "parallel city" is the site of this bookstore which makes it even more legible by mimicking the parallel spatial structure of its larger context.

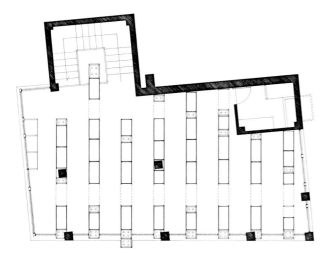

Second storey plan

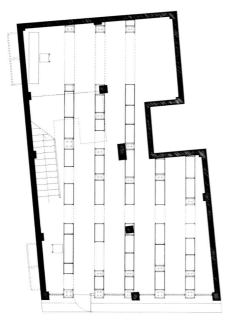

First storey plan

Pictograph DenCity

Traffic DenCity
Xishu Bookstore. Beijing. 1996.

The bookstore occupies what once was a passageway in a 1950s office complex. Its other original passageway remains a busy traffic corridor, always filled with bicycles. The site analysis leads to the design of a hybrid object nicknamed book-bike, which marries bookshelves to ready-made bike wheels. The book-bikes enable the shelves to revolve around the circular steel columns, which support the mezzanine floor above, and the motion of bike wheels suggests the flow of street traffic into the store. In other words, the bookstore becomes an extension of the larger urban space. On a practical level, the book-bikes provide spatial flexibility.

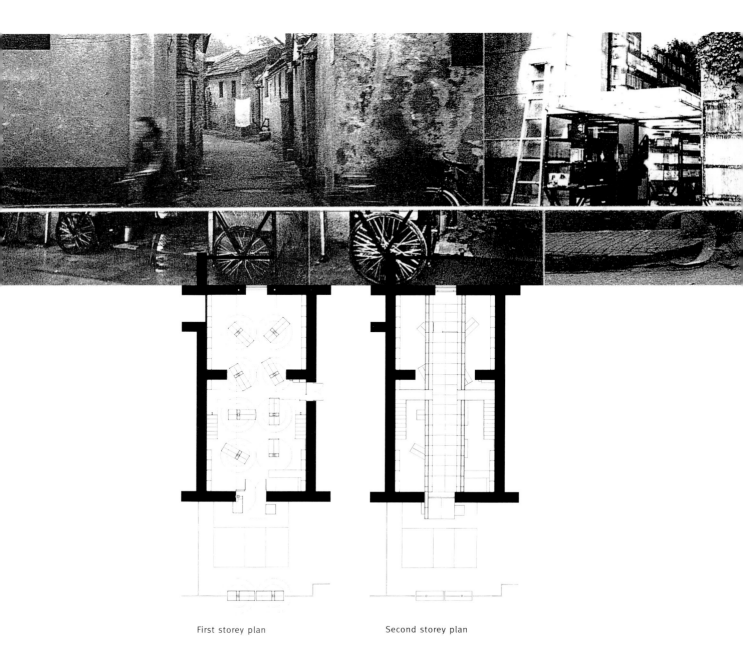

First storey plan   Second storey plan

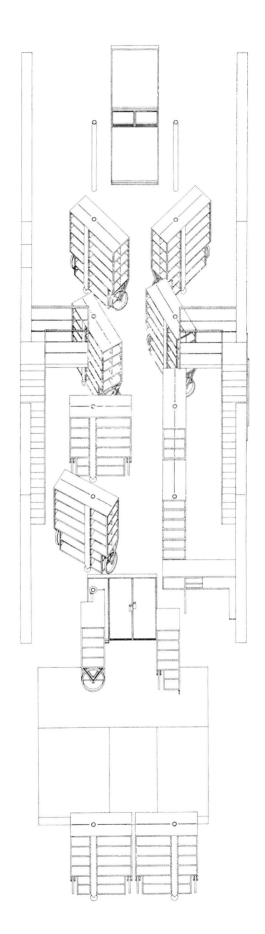

View of mezzanine.

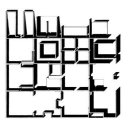

Entrance to bookshop with book-bike doors.

Vertical DenCity
'Upside Down Office' Cummins Asia Headquarters, Beijing, 1997.

There has been always the need for two offices: One that is private and minimises distractions and the other that is open and encourages communication and team work. The traditional work cubicle, however, provides one the first office at the expense of natural light and view and the second office, which is usually defined by open space, only when he/she goes for a coffee or to the toilet. With the analysis, the reversal of what is typically open and enclosed presents a solution: In this office, the workstations are partitioned with glass curtain walls that are transparent on the lower half and translucent on the upper. Therefore, one sees through the entire office once sitting down to work and will regain the room thus his/her privacy when he/she gets up for a break. The design could be perceived as two thin architectures, 1.3 meters each with one open and one enclosed, stacked up in one 2.6-meter floor. The anti-cubicle approach turns the traditional open office upside down.

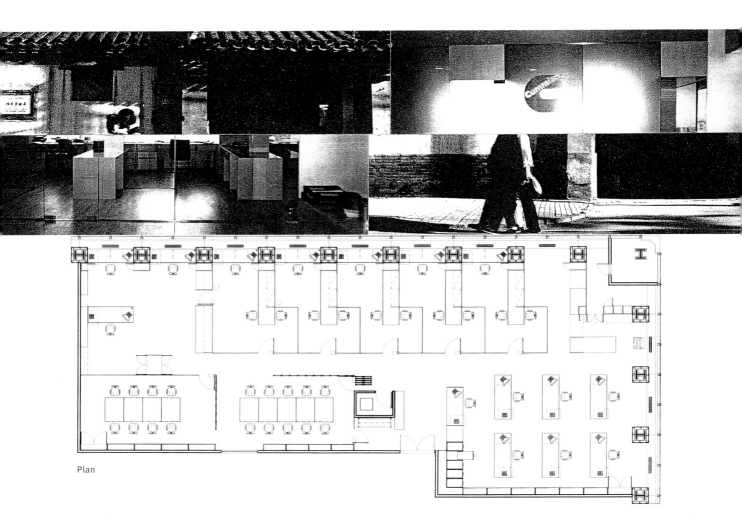

Plan

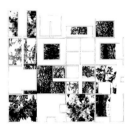

Pictograph DenCity

Building DenCity

Morningside Centre of Mathematics, Chinese Academy of Sciences, Beijing, 1998.

In the design of this research complex, the idea of dense-urbanism is translated into a miniature city. The programme asks for a singular structure on a tight site to accommodate all the daily activities of the mathematicians except dining. This living-working arrangement refuses the researchers the opportunity to go into the city. In order to bring only a vague sense of urban living to the center's residents, a city has to be created inside the building. The seven-storey edifice is therefore dissolved into five internal buildings according to their different uses. The miniature towers are defined by different architectural qualities: private spaces, as in the individual research tower and the dormitory tower, open on one side, while the tower containing the public spaces is open on two opposite sides; and semi-public spaces, also forming a separate stack, are translucent on two opposite sides. The mini-towers are then connected with passages, light wells, and bridges over a sky-lit gap. The gap may be seen as a traditional Chinese courtyard only squeezed tightly to fit in the contemporary Asian city. By such a design, it is hoped that one may blur the experience of going from one room to another with that of going from building to building.

Entrance with ramp for handicapped; passage with translucent glass walls; translucent passage and transparent public space open to terrace.

View from northeast

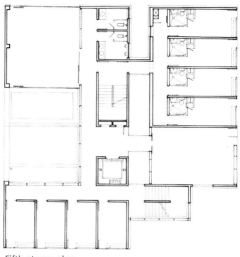

Fifth storey plan

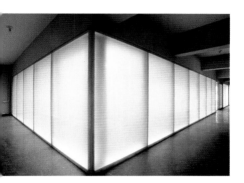

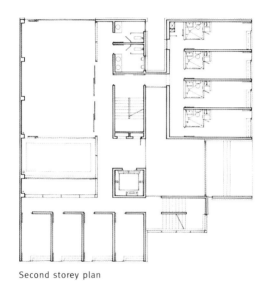

Second storey plan

Pictograph DenCity

First storey plan

0   5   10m

Courtyard DenCity
Hillside Housing in Qingxi, Guangdong. 1995.

The hillside suburban housing project tries to interpret the spatial traditions of the Chinese house. While the typical Chinese house is always hollow in the centre, courtyards in the south are considerably smaller than the northern ones to shade off excessive sunshine. Each Qingxi house is built around a sequence of small courtyards or "sky-wells" as in the vernacular architecture of the area, to accommodate the time-honoured local habit of outdoor living, but with contemporary construction materials and methods. The Qingxi house becomes a traditional dwelling without the traditional look. And as row houses, the Qingxi project consolidates the open spaces and defies the peripheral yards of American suburbia.

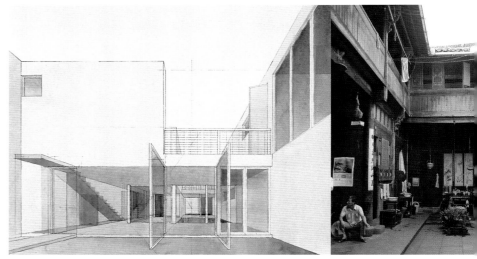

Left: House B from courtyard.   Right: Sky-well in vernacular house.

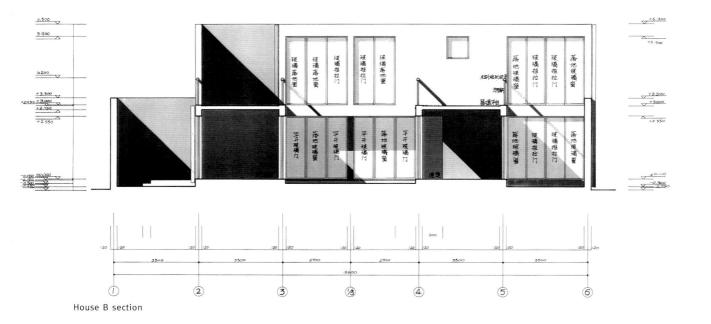

House B section

Pictograph DenCity

Park/hotel in Humen. Guangdong. 1995 (unbuilt).

In the Chinese script, enclosed space is signified by an empty rectangular frame. The reading of Chinese pictographs as spatial diagrams initiated the design of this park/hotel. The study of words evolves into a morphological inquiry of courtyards. Sixteen ideograms/courtyards are arranged onto the building site to respond conceptually to a classic poem capturing the scenic quality of local ocean front and programmatically to the complex requirements of the park and the hotel. Among the facilities of hospitality is a group of suite towers freestanding in the landscape connected by an elevated driveway.

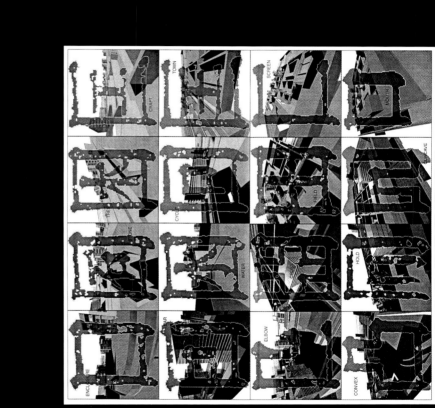

Looking north

First floor

Second floor

Conclusion

The density of city develops in both macro and micro directions. In Asia where extreme urban density becomes a common phenomenon, one often finds oneself living simultaneously in a big metropolis and a small self-sufficient enclave. While the metropolis expands constantly, can the enclave shrink infinitely? However, the question is not about how small the city can be but how dense it may become. In the juxtaposition of the macro and micro densities, building design looses its validity as the departure of architectural practice. Any building design, regardless of its size, is thus urban design and about urbanism. For now, and for us, however, it's all about Dense Urbanism.

Architecture moves us.

It evokes emotive responses at every moulding of its shapes, at every change of space, at the subt[le] change of light and at the transformation of texture and materials. We make architecture out of the passion that it expresses, out [of] our learning, our hidden subconscious, out of our very own soul. Architecture for us is a visual and phenomenological experienc[e] which generally needs no literary and verbal description. It needs only to be seen and experienced.

It is derived from the initial slashing and meandering of lines across paper, done intuitively from preliminary briefs. In recent year[s] various starting precepts have become more obvious, particularly where lines could be inflected to achieve curved planes an[d] changing tones of light, and also when various shapes could be turned into components, creating interstitial spaces where the[y] intersect.

While working with abstraction in this manner, we feel that after the initial intuitive gesture, every line drawn and built must b[e] supported by reasons, each line becomes a deliberate act. At every opportunity, we would choose to mould shapes, we would te[ll] stories with our forms and carve our experiences out of our spaces. We would investigate how natural light changes in tone at eve[ry] curve and at every turn. We would create shadows out of projections and turn walls into etchings.

Each building becomes a[n] essay, grammatically correct, telling stories appropriate to its particular time and place.

We are influenced by all the Modernist masters and also by all contemporary works of architecture. Most of all, we admire th[e] thoughts and works of Le Corbusier.

In today's global environment, we do not feel the need to consciously worry about working in an identifiably Asian context. W[e] believe in abstraction because it provides freedom from such consternation. We respond to our climatic conditions because th[is] provides reasons for our forms and we believe in technology because we can only move forward.

Because we are Asian an[d] we live and behave like Asians, our architecture becomes Asian.

Lim Teng Ngiom

Architecture as Lyrical Essays

PKLC
Port Klang. Malaysia
1996.

The PKLC project is one amongst a series of projects which has its formal basis derived from the idea of "inflection". Located at an intersection in a rather grim and remote industrial estate, the project provides both a visual relief to the staid environmental and serves as a marker at the intersection.

The project is essentially made up of a logistic warehouse at the back with an area of approximately 7,800 sq m and an operations office of 750 sq m in front. The building is constructed entirely of steel on concrete plinth.

The operations office at the front is expressed with metal sheets, spanning over 30 m. To preserve the integrity of the concept and to maintain the purity of form it is important that the inflected sectional line remains unbroken.

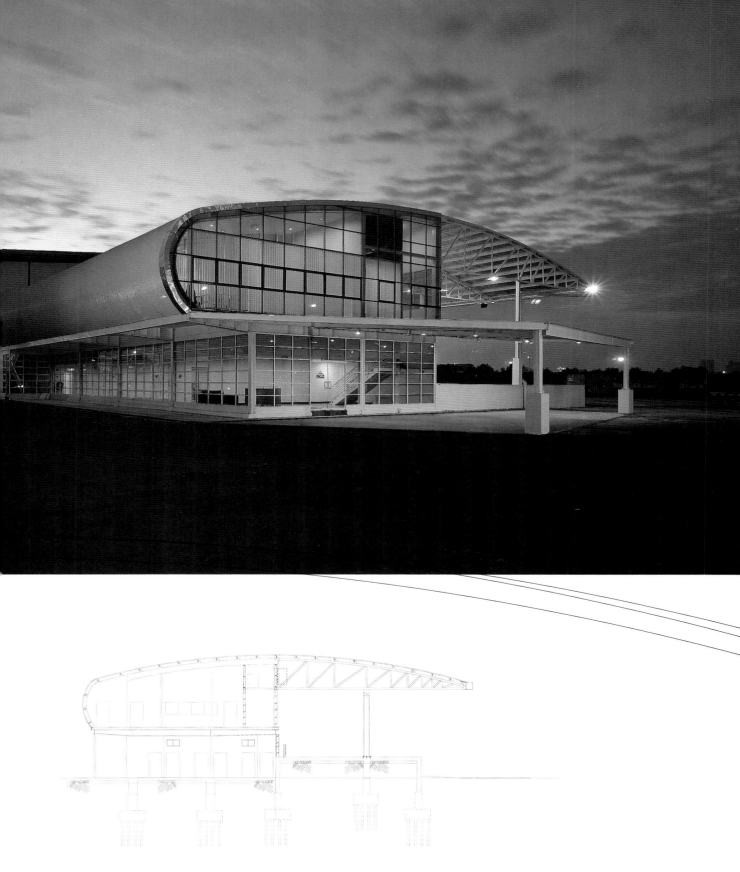

Section through office

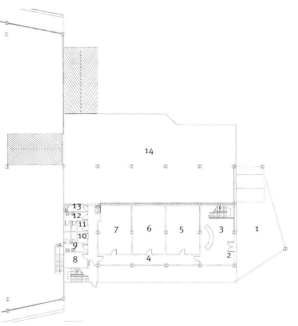

Ground floor plan

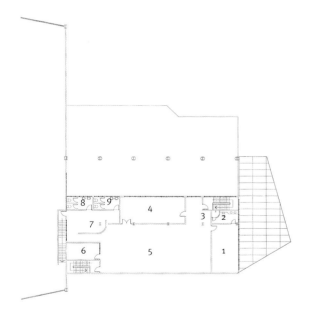

First floor plan

1	Porte cochere	8	Switch room
2	Waiting	9	Female toilet
3	Reception	10	Surau
4	Walkway	11	Surau
5	Office	12	Male toilet
6	Office	13	Tearoom
7	Office	14	Loading/unloading dock

1	Director's room	8	Male toilet
2	Ensuite bathroom	9	Female toilet
3	Reception		
4	Conference		
5	Office		
6	Office		
7	Pantry		

Wisma Laju

Shah Alam, Malaysia

1998.

Wisma Laju is part of a series of work that relies on abstraction to achieve lyricism where light is used to sculpt form and space. The location of the building in the tropics determined that shaded terraces be provided to enable users to gain relief from the air-conditioned interior. The two main garden terraces punctuate the building at the highest and intermediate levels. They provide spatial links between the inside and the outside. For a small building, it supports three different functions: a product assembly area at the ground floor, an apartment at the top floor and offices in the intermediate zone. The building was designed on an existing structural platform where concrete footings and piles were already completed according to a previous design. The construction took a total of only nine months.

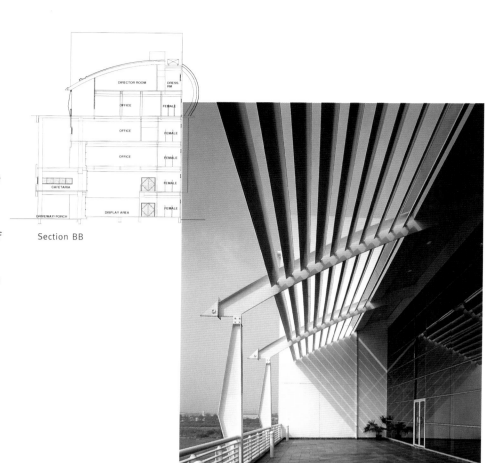

Section BB

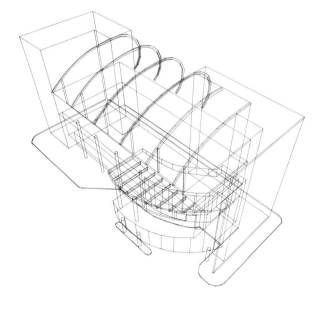

Pat's House

Sungai Buloh. Malaysia
1999.

Done in the spirit of the
early Modernists, the
house is an expression of
pure function, a "machine
for living." The shape of
the house is determined
by its use, the constraints
of a low budget and
available views. There is
also a conscious effort in
achieving fluidity in
space, where spaces flow
with the topography of
the land. The house is a
single extended platform
which is inflected in the
middle as it pulls itself
over the gently sloping
terrain.

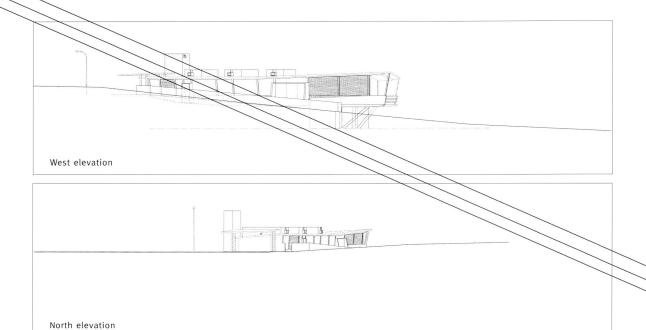

West elevation

North elevation

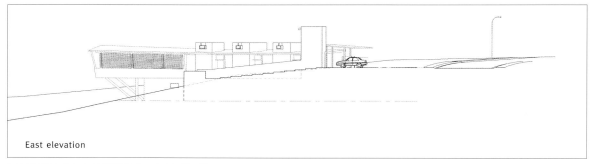

East elevation

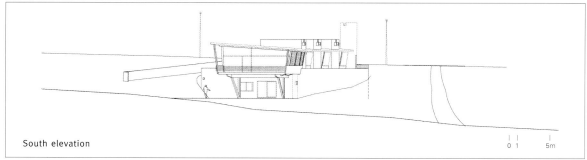

South elevation

0 1   5m

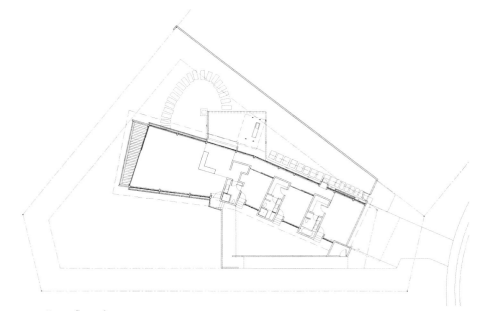

Upper floor plan

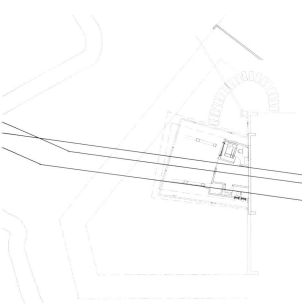

Lower floor plan

0 1   5m

Sean Godsell

Simplicity

The common ground in the works is unquestionably 'simplicity'. My designs emerge from an innate desire for order and I derive enormous satisfaction from being able to draw the most basic diagram which illustrates the solution to a complex problem. Equal to my desire for order is my interest in the complexities of people and the societies they attempt to construct. My work therefore constantly ebbs and flows between logical, rational problem solving and deliberate spatial complexity. The architecture which results, achieves what Matisse describes as "beauty through contrast" and what Lao Tzu calls the essential void.

The MacSween House is a good example of spatial complexity achieved within a simple format. Upon entering the house a visitor is confronted with one space which constitutes the entire ground floor. Drawn into the house by two level changes and a view to the distant courtyard (a simple picturesque device employed first by Capability Brown and later refined by Lutyens) visitors find themselves quite quickly at the back door. At the apparent end of their journey but with no obvious way upstairs, the visitors are forced to retrace their steps until they discover the stairs, at the front of the house but concealed from view. The simplicity of the rectangular plan is deliberately used to contrast with a spatial complexity which is not at first evident to the visitor. It is the drama which results from this basic strategy that enlivens all of the works in this volume.

"A great opportunity is yours. The occasion confronts you. The future is in your hands – will you accept the responsibility or will you evade it. That is the only vital question I have to put to you. Do you intend or do you not intend, do you wish or do you not wish, to become architects to whose care an unfolding democracy may entrust the interpretation of its material wants, its psychic aspirations?"

Louis Sullivan, 1900

My buildings also display a reverence for the mathematical order inherent in nature. As architects the tangible means of composition available to us are limited by technology, however the transformations of these compositions offered by nature are limitless. When a painter makes a picture, his work is designed to be viewed under consistent, static, gallery light. When an architect designs, he must consider the way all types of light will model and shape the building. In the Kew House I have set up a conceptual framework that enables the simple to become complex without resorting to complicated devices. The building is a rectangle, in both plan and elevation. The façade is veiled with a system of adjustable louvres which blur the edge of the building and constantly modify its appearance depending upon the position of the viewer. This is a conscious attempt to accentuate the buoyancy of the intermittent changes caused by changing light conditions, without which clarity and obscurity would not exist. Light enters or is prevented from entering the building in a constantly changing way, modifying the appearance of materials and the moods of the occupants as it does so. Nature itself acts in this way – continually making and unmaking, filling and emptying.

The limitations of budget (which are also a constant in the enclosed work) enhance and at times enforce simple design decision-making. Structure and material become the decorative elements – pragmatism in issues such as environmental design wins out over embellishments, detailing is deliberately low-key rather than arrogant. This utilitarianism, combined with the complex spatial treatment described gives my work an edginess, a rawness which ensures that visitors are never seduced by the object itself (a superficial outcome) but rather by their own capacity to experience the potential of the human spirit.

MacSween House

Melbourne. Australia.

1995.

This building is situated in the Lynch's Bridge Development of the Melbourne CBD. The brief was to design a small house for a single person in his early thirties. The steel frame is expressed and the beams extend beyond the façade to the north and south, implying a universal infinite grid of portal frames of which the house, by virtue of its walls and roof, becomes a part. The walls are white painted cement rendered over a stud frame. It is the roof however which dominates the composition. The barge board is 400 mm wide, dressed in Oregon, while the soffit is sawn cedar. The massiveness of the roof is accentuated by cutting the barge board horizontal to the ground and eliminating the gutters. A series of steel portal frames combined with prefabricated trusses enable speed of construction compared to conventional house building techniques which involve working from the ground up. This has two main advantages – the work area is sheltered early in the construction sequence therefore reducing the likelihood of time lost due to wet weather.

Inside, the plywood (second-hand ply used for making crates) is left raw and uncoated. Both its surface defects and its patchwork of pink primer colour theme are used for the door to the guest bedroom (pink) and the front door (orange). At the top of the stairs the green box projects into the stairwell and reflects the colour of the battered grass embankment outside. The concrete floor is left as it was poured. The timber beams are exposed in part and the steel connections are bolted – drawing from the 'anti architectural' of the industrial box.

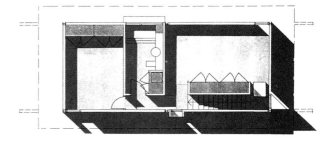

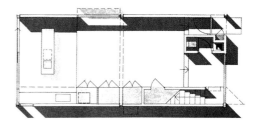

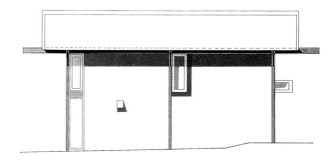

Kew House
Melbourne, 1997.

The house is 18 m by 9 m and cantilevers 5.5 m over a steep slope at the west end of the site. It is constructed from 350 mmpa steel which is oxidised and then sealed with a clear primer. The house is divided length-ways. To the north, an open-plan living space, to the south interconnecting bedrooms and a study. A 7 m built in table runs across the east end of the building and has been designed as the hub of daily life in the home. The plan is 'Eastern' – one space divided and there are no corridors. The sentiment of the kitchen table is 'Western' – the altar of the family. In this sense the house specu-lates on the potential of the Australian vernacular, born not simply from our European past but equally from our acceptance of our regional reality as part of Asia.

The site slopes steeply to the west. The building ignores the slope and addresses the view to the city skyline. The heroic nature of the structure defers to the post-war optimism of Melbourne architecture evidenced in suburbs such as Kew, North Balwyn and Beaumaris.

Although apparently 'modern' in its language, the house is primordial in its intent – rust, oiled second-hand boards, recycled decking and a lack of 'precious' detail combine with rudimentary services to form a house which is elemental rather than processed.

Operable steel shutters shade the north and west elevations. A passive evaporative cooling system takes the prevailing southwesterly wind over the grass embankment and under the house where it is introduced via floor vents to the east end of the building. The air is further cooled by fine water mist sprays placed at the top end of the embankment.

1999

Carter/Tucker House

Breamlea, Victoria, completed 2000.

A three level 12 m x 6 m box was embedded into the side of a sand dune. The house has three rooms. The lower ground floor is for guests and the single space can be divided by a sliding wall into two rooms if so required. Similarly, the single space on the middle level can also be divided to separate the owners' bedroom from a small sitting area. The top floor is for living and eating and takes advantage of views across a rural landscape. It is also a daylight photographic studio.

In traditional Chinese architecture, the aisle is a fluid outer building continuous around the perimeter of the inner building. In traditional Japanese architecture, the aisle (gejin) is not continuous when added to a structure (hisashi) but is fluid space when an inner building is partitioned (hedate) to cause an aisle to be formed. The traditional outback Australian homestead is also surrounded by fluid space (verandah) which is sometimes partly enclosed with fly-wire or glass to form an indoor/outdoor space (sunroom). In the outback the verandah helped shade the vertical surfaces of the building from direct solar radiation. In both eastern and western examples the verandah provided transitional living space. The Carter/Tucker house is primarily an investigation of the verandah/aisle and its potential as an iconic element common between eastern and western architecture; a response to the evolving dynamic of Australia's European history and regional reality.

The verandah exists in this house in an abstract form. In has been analysed and then re-created using a process similar to that which Braques and Picasso employed in their Analytical (first stage) Cubist paintings of last century. In other words, elements of the object exist throughout the building. However, its traditional form is not immediately evident. On all three levels the outer (timber screen) skin of the building tilts open and by tilting an awning is formed on the perimeter of the building. The horizontal plane of the ceiling is thus extended beyond the building line. At the same time, the apparently flat façade of the building is modified in an arbitrary manner as a result of the owners' particular requirement for view and shade at any given time. The (capricious) component allows the fluidity of the aisle space to transfer itself across the façade of the building and the very act of inhabitation means that the façade becomes a dynamic representation of the plan. On the middle level for example the bedroom then becomes the verandah while the corridor, formed by the insertion of a service core, becomes the inner room. Depending on the time of the year the verandah can then be enclosed with sliding fly-screens to become a sunroom, or left un-enclosed. The bedroom space can then be further modified by the operation of the hedate wall which when drawn across the bedroom forms an inner building within the aisle. The idea of fluid space is further emphasised by the service core being kept free from both ends of the building so that movement through the floor is continuous – no steps have to be retraced.

By describing the three rooms of this building as aisles and therefore by definition transitional, I am also alert to the fact that this is a weekend house, not a permanent dwelling. There is invested in this building a strong sense of childhood that begins with the anticipation of travel and promotes the sense of reward that comes at the conclusion of a journey. In a recent visit to Paris, I re-visited Le Corbusier's Roche/Jeanneret house and was reminded as to where I had first encountered some fifteen years ago that same idea of journey, discovery and reward in architecture.

Finally, there is a raw humanity to this building which is first evidenced in the MacSween house (1998) and further developed in the Kew house. In both this building and the Kew house, the façades are veiled with a system of adjustable louvres which blurs the edges of the building and constantly modify its appearance depending upon the position of the viewer. This is a conscious attempt to accentuate the buoyancy of intermittent light changes caused by changing light conditions, without which clarity and obscurity would not exist. Light enters or is prevented from entering the building in a constantly changing way. Nature itself acts in this manner – constantly making and unmaking, filling and emptying. The entire building has been designed to weather – to allow the inevitability of the environment and time to play a positive role. This rawness also ensures that the visitor is never seduced by the object itself (a superficial outcome) but rather by their own capacity to experience the potential of the human spirit.

Art Faculty
St. Paul's School
Baxter, Victoria.
1998.

This is an addition to
the existing Art Faculty.
The new work unfolds
from the existing and
uses circulation space as
gallery space for students'
paintings, sculptures
and photographs.
A corner of the circulation
space is set aside
for installation art.
As the building unfolds
(west façade) it re-
organises itself (south
façade) and becomes
an ordered and
coherent response to
the programme.

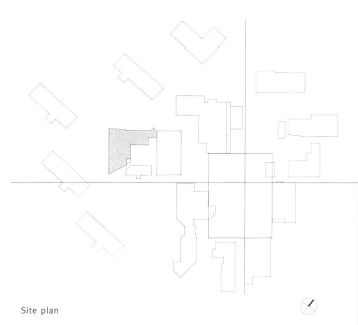

Site plan

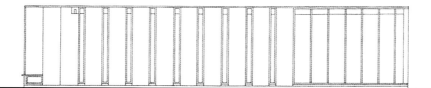

Elevation

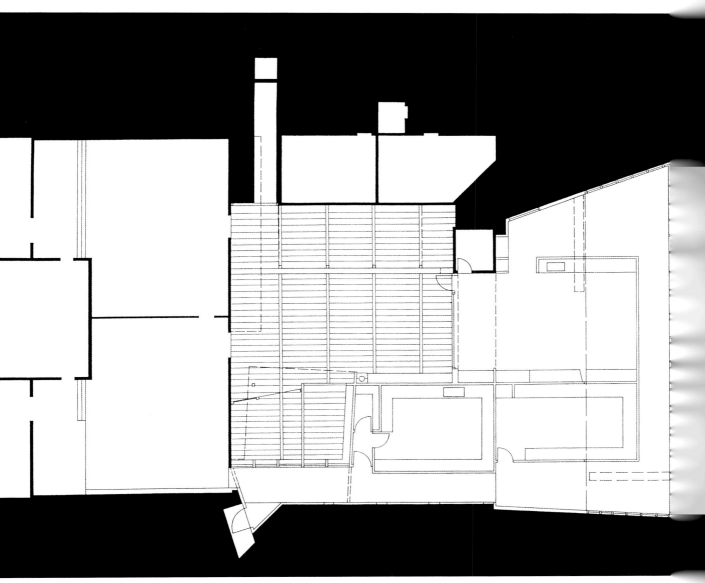

Plan

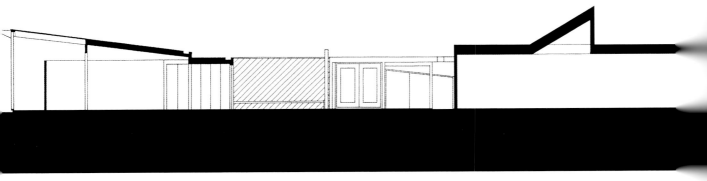

Section

Biodata

Kenneth Frampton

Kenneth Frampton trained as an architect at the Architectural Association School of Architecture, London. He has worked as an architect and as an architectural historian/critic in England, Israel and the United States. He is currently the Ware Professor of Architecture at the Graduate School of Architecture, Planning and Preservation at Columbia University, New York. His books include *Modern Architecure: a Critical History* (1980), *Modern Architecture and the Critical Present* (1980), *Studies in Tectonic Culture* (1995) and *American Masterworks* (1995).

Gülsüm Baydar
Nalbantoglu (b.1956)

Dr. Gülsüm Baydar Nalbantoglu received her doctorate from University of California, Berkeley in 1989. She has taught in several universities including University of California, Berkeley (1984-89), University of California, Santa Cruz (1988-1990) and the School of Architecture, National University of Singapore (1990-1997). She is currently associate professor at Bilkent University, Department of Interior Architecture and Environmental Design. Her many essays and articles are published in journals such as *Assemblage* and she is the co-editor of *Postcolonial Space*(s) (Princeton Architectural Press, 1997).

Paul Carter
(b. 1951)

Professor Paul Carter is a writer and artist whose books include *Lost Subjects* and *Depth of Translation, The book of Raft* (both 1999), *The Lie of the Land* (1996), *Living In A New Country* (1992) and *The Road to Botany Bay* (1987). Jadi Jadian, a performance-based heritage design in Georgetown, Penang, forms part of a five year research program called Ephemeral Architectures, supported by the Australian Research Council. He is Professorial Research Fellow at The Australian Centre, University of Melbourne and adjunct professor within the Faculty of Constructed Environment, Royal Melbourne Institute of Technology, Melbourne.

Geoffrey Bawa
(b. 1919)

After graduating with a law degree from Cambridge, Bawa embarked on his architectural training at the Architectural Association in London, graduating in 1956. After a long and luminous career as an architect in Sri Lanka, and having won many important architectural awards, he was conferred the title "Vidya Jothi" (Light of Science) in 1985, and the title "Deshamanya" (Pride of the Nation) in 1993 by the President of Sri Lanka. His works have been exhibited at the RIBA in London as well as in New York, Boston, Singapore, Sao Paulo, Belo Horizonte, Australia, and Colombo.

Tao Ho
(b. 1936)

Tao Ho is the immediate past president of the Hong Kong Institute of Architects. A native Cantonese but born in Shanghai in 1936, his education included the Chinese classics, a degree in art history from Williams College Massachusetts and a master's in architecture from Harvard. He was personal assistant to Walter Gropius and Siegfried Giedion before returning to Hong Kong in 1964. Taoho Design Architects provides urban design, architecture and interior design services in Hong Kong, mainland China and internationally. Tao Ho is also actively engaged in other arts and cultural activities. He has received many awards recognising his contributions to architecture and to international understanding.

Ernesto Bedmar
(b. 1954)

Since qualifying in 1980 from the University of Cordoba in Argentina, Ernesto Bedmar has worked with Miguel Angel Roca, directing his overseas offices in Africa and Asia. In Singapore since the establishment of Bedmar & Shi Design in 1986, he has been responsible for various types of projects including the Dover Park Hospice, private residences, and shophouse conservation projects. He has also been a part-time lecturer in the School of Architecture, National University of Singapore for the past eight years.

Charles Correa
(b. 1930)

Charles Correa began his practice as an architect in Bombay in 1958. He has done pioneering work on urban issues and low-cost shelter in many countries and has won many awards including the Aga Khan Award for Architecture (1988) and gold medals from IUA, IIA and RIBA. He has also taught at various universities in India, the United States, and the United Kingdom.

Seung Hchioh Sang
(b. 1952)

After receiving his bachelor's and master's degrees from Seoul National University, he worked for Space Group of Korea, founded by the late Kim Swoo Geun from 1974 to 1989. Since 1989, he has been in independent practice. He received the KIA prizes in 1991, 1992, the Kim Swoo Geun Prize in 1993, and the Grand Prize of Architectural Culture in 1993. He has been a studio critic at Hanyang, Kyungki, Ehwa and Seoul National University, and a guest lecturer at the AA School in London.

Rahul Mehrotra	William S. W. Lim	Nevzat Sayin	Chang Yung Ho
(b. 1959)	(b. 1932)	(b. 1954)	(b. 1956)

Rahul Mehrotra
(b. 1959)

He received a diploma in architecture from the School of Architecture, Ahmedabad, and in 1987 received a master's in Urban Design from Harvard University. After working with Charles Correa in Bombay for two years, he founded Rahul Mehrotra Associates in 1990. Over the last six years, the practice has been involved in projects which include interior design, urban design, conservation, and restoration of historic buildings. Mehrotra is the executive director of the Urban Design Research Institute in Bombay which promotes research on the city with the aim of influencing urban planning policy.

William S. W. Lim
(b. 1932)

A graduate of the Architectural Association (AA) London, he continued his graduate study at the Department of City and Regional Planning, Harvard University, as a Fullbright Fellow. He is the principal partner of William Lim Associates whose main focus is idea innovation and design excellence. Lim writes and lectures. His recent books are: *Asian New Urbanism* (1998), *Contemporary Vernacular: Evoking Traditions in Asian Architecture* (1998). Lim is the president of AA Asia, a board member of LaSalle-SIA College of Fine Arts (Singapore) and an editorial board member of Solidarity: current affairs, ideas and the arts (Manila). He is also adjunct professor of the RMIT, Australia and guest professor at Tianjin University, China.

Nevzat Sayin
(b. 1954)

Nevrat Sayin graduated in 1978 from the Department of Architecture, Aegean University in Izmir.
He started his own studio in 1984 and has received several awards including the National Architectural Awards by the Turkish Chamber of Architects of Istanbul and the Turkish Association of Freelance Architects Award. He has been at design juries at various schools of architecture in Ankara, Bursa, Istanbul and Eskisehir.

Chang Yung Ho
(b. 1956)

He obtained his basic architectural training from Nanjing Institute of Technology and Ball State University before graduating with a master's in architecture from Univeristy of California at Berkeley. He has won several international competitions including Japan Architect's Shinkenchiku Residential Design Competition in 1986 and received the Progressive Architecture Citiation Award in 1995. A monograph of the work of his practice Atelier Feichang Jianzhu was published in 1997 in China. He was assistant professor at Rice University from 1993 to 1996.

Lim Teng Ngiom
(b. 1955)

Lim Teng Ngiom completed
his architectural education at
the University of North
London. He was the editor of
the *Malaysian Architect*
between 1991-1995, and has
published numerous
architectural essays locally
and abroad. He is active in
practice and in architectural
education. In 1995, he was
instrumental in setting up
the school of architecture in
the University of Malaya.

Sean Godsell
(b. 1960)

Sean Godsell was born
in Melbourne in 1960.
He graduated with first class
honours from The University
of Melbourne in 1984.
He worked in London from
1986 to 1988 for Sir Denys
Lasdun. In 1989 he returned
to Melbourne and com-
menced private practice.
In 1994 he formed Godsell
Associates Pty Ltd Architects.
He obtained a master's of
architecture degree from
RMIT University in 1999.

Tan Kok Meng
(b. 1964)

Tan Kok Meng graduated
from the School of Architecture, National University of
Singapore in 1992 and a
Masters in Architecture and
Urban Culture from UPC
(Barcelona). He has been a
part-time lecturer at both
RMIT/LaSalle-SIA College of
the Arts (Interior Architecture)
and the National University
of Singapore. Currently, he
is the chief editor of the
Singapore Architect journal.

A reliable, proficient main contractor
for the avant-garde, exciting

Marine Parade Community Club

We are committed to provide quality
Services that meet our clients' needs and satisfaction

STILE

... stone & tile showroom

tiles • glass mosaics • silica agglomerates • granite • quartzites • marbles • sandstone • limestone • pebbles • laminated floors • sealers & stonecare products

S T I L E... stone & tile showroom 11 changi south street 3 builders centre #04 - 01 singapore 486122 tel 545 5225 fax 545 5665 email sales@buildersshop.com.sg

S T I L E... created by  BUILDERS SHOP
鲁班行

Egner Building Technologies Pte. Ltd
ARCHITECTURAL METAL ROOF- AND WALL CLADDING

* Tudor Ten, Singapore
Bedmar & Shi Designers Pte Ltd and B&S&T Architects

** Watten Estate Singapore
WOHA Designs

** Peh Residence, Singapore
SCDA-Architects

*** Changi Mosque, Singapore
Alfred Wong Partnership Architects

We specialised in design, supply and installation of Custom made Metal Roof and Metal Wall Cladding, in standing seam (25mm high locked seam) and flat seam quality. All fixing parts are consealed.
<u>We are using the following materials:-</u>

- (**)   Classic Copper TECU®
- (***)   Patina Copper TECU®
-          Tin-coated copper TECU®
-          Oxide copper TECU®
- (*)   PvdF2 colour coated Aluminium Faizonal®
-          Tin-coated stainless steel UGINOX AME®
-          Other specialist roof-and wall claddings works and materials

We are working internationally on high-end properties.

 Egner Building Technologies Pte. Ltd
Specialist roofing contractor

10 Anson Road, #10-06 International Plaza, Singapore 079903
Tel: (65) 324 1119 / 743 3691 Fax: (65) 743 3692
E-mail: egnerblg@mbox5.singnet.com.sg
Web site: www.roofmetal.com

Acknowledgements

Photo Credits	Page
Gülsüm B. Nalbantoglu	23
Leon van Schaik	30 (top)
Paul Carter	35
Jim Hooper	36 (bottom)
Xiao Photo Workshop	87-95
Tan Kah Heng	96-101, 158 (1st & 2nd from left), 160-166
Dinesh Mehta	106 (2nd from left), 107
Mahendra Sinh	106 (3rd from left)
Rahul Mehrotra	106 (4th from left), 109 (top right), 112 (bottom 3rd from left), 116-117, 119 (2nd from left), 138, 144-147, 149
Rohinton Irani	112 (2nd from left), 114-115 (bottom), 119 (1st from left)
Kim Jaekyung	136
Rajesh Vora	142-147
Ajay Mirajgaoker	149
Brent Bear/Impact	154 (2nd from left)
R.Ian Lloyd	157 (2nd from right)
Teh Joo Heng	158 (3rd from left)
Tang Gaun Bee	159
E. Carter	226 (top), 228-229
Sean Godsell	226 (bottom)
T. Mein	227
Dorothy Alexander	234 (Kenneth Frampton's photo)
Angela Bailey	234 (Paul Carter's photo)

The publisher also wishes to thank the architects, photographers, sponsors and all who have contributed so much to make this publication possible.